Just a boy from Bristol

Michael J. Kelly

ISBN: 1503020037
ISBN-13: 9781503020030

DEDICATION

To my mother who inspired me to read, to write and to love.

CONTENTS

ACKNOWLEDGMENTS

My wife, my rock, for her patient and constant support.

MT, my editor, who was an immense help in the production of my book.

1 THROUGH THE EYES OF A CHILD

On the 3rd September 1939 a war started that would not only change the course of history, it would also deny millions of children across the world the opportunity for a normal, happy childhood. I know, because I was one of them.

My father, who had spent the bulk of his adult life in the Royal Navy, re-enlisted as soon as the storm clouds of war started to gather over Europe. He left my mother alone, to bring up two young children, in poverty, and in what was becoming a scary, changing world.

My mother was an incredibly beautiful young woman, but she was emotionally fragile. She was an, unpredictable, free spirited, capricious butterfly, who was constantly fluttering around; she was never able to settle anywhere for long. In many ways she was totally unsuited to the task in hand, but she was a mother, and she did what mothers do best. She cared for me; she did it well, and I will be eternally grateful to her. Mum, I thank you for teaching me how to live and how to love. I thank you for the incredible journey, and I thank you for all the many wonderful memories.

I was only two when my father went off to war. I was far too young to have any memories of him. All that I had was a small, crumpled photograph, which showed him as a young man wearing football kit. He had scribbled a message on the back.

I won't be long, don't worry, because I will be lucky.
Joe

That photograph was to live behind the clock, on the mantle shelf of whichever house we were living in for the duration of the war. Whenever the going got too tough, which was often, Mum would take it down and read the message aloud to me. I think it was probably as much for her benefit as it was for mine.

My earliest memories are of the spring of 1940. I was still a few months short of my third birthday, but my memories, although few, are very clear. We were living like three rats, in a tiny ground floor flat in Badminton Road, St Paul's. The house was right on the junction of Ashley Road, Lower Ashley Road and Sussex Place. I shared a double bed with my mother, and my baby sister Mary slept in her pushchair, under the window in the cramped living room area. I envied Mary's ability to sleep. It would stand her in good stead later on when the German bombers flew over Bristol.

The actual fighting hadn't reached Bristol yet, but the effects of the war certainly had. The strict rationing meant a shortage of food, and in our case, there was always a shortage of money. There were frequent trips to the pawn shop, and there were ration books, blackouts at night, gas masks to carry, and frequent air raid drills. Despite all this, life carried on remarkably normally. We all got by somehow, and we all survived. Whenever shops had food supplies, the rumours spread like wild fire and the housewives would queue for miles. I think in a funny sort of way, the women quite enjoyed those long queues, and they would gossip away contentedly as they waited for their turns.

My first, my best, and my only friend, was Mrs. Grant who lived across the road. Mrs. Grant was a formidable looking Irish woman. She was short, sturdy and permanently wore a flowered pinafore and a hairnet, which covered an army of rather vicious looking metal curlers. She may have been a woman, but she still had whiskers, warts and muscles. I had already decided if and when the Germans ever invaded Badminton Road, I would hide behind Mrs. Grant. Those curlers would be more than a match for anything the Germans could throw at us.

Mrs. Grant and I had a simple, but very effective relationship. She gave me food in the form of biscuits, cakes, sweets and sausage sandwiches; in return, I satisfied her curiosity by answering her many questions and supplying her with information about my mother. The questions would come at me thick and fast.

"Where was your mother going yesterday afternoon?" "Where did you last live?" "Do you remember your father?" "How old is your mother? How old is your father?"

I could tell her nothing, because I didn't know the answer to any of her questions, but I valued those extra rations, and to keep her happy I would fabricate stories about my mother's movements, her past life and her future intentions. It all seemed to work rather well, and I lived in my own idyllic world where I could have both a full stomach and a clear conscience.

The highlight of my week was a Sunday morning when the Salvation Army band came a-calling. They would always stop at the top of the road and belt out a couple of big, brassy numbers. It was my first taste of live music, and its appeal has never left me. I was fascinated by all the instruments and the musicians. In particular, I was taken with the big bass drum and the drummer. It was a very big drum, and the drummer was a very large man with a florid complexion and a bushy black moustache. For the final leg of the journey back to the Citadel, I would march alongside him. I held my left index finger across my upper lip to simulate his moustache; I puffed out my cheeks to simulate his size and with my free right hand, I would air drum like a maniac. Boom! Boom! Boom!

When the show was finally over, I would trudge slowly home. It seems inconceivable in this day and age, but there I was, yet to reach the age of three, and I was already wandering around St Paul's all alone and unattended. I knew no fear, because I didn't see myself as a young child and, in any event, I considered the area bounded by the triangle of Brigstocke Road, Ashley Road and City Road to be my manor; it was my hood, and I strutted around those streets like a miniature boss.

It was around about this time I learnt my first harsh lesson in life. I learnt that nothing good lasts forever. It was a warm April afternoon, and Mum, Mary, the pushchair and I headed down to St James Churchyard. This is now the site of the Primark store, but was then a triangular, concrete surfaced park. There was a weighbridge, a few scattered benches and, what felt like a million pigeons. I would wander amongst those birds, scattering stale bread crumbs for them. They were very tame, and it gave me a great sense of power.

On this particular day I had run out of bread crumbs and I turned to Mum for reinforcements. To my shock, she was talking to a man;

a complete stranger. He was a tall, thin man, with very white teeth. Apart from a white collarless shirt, he was dressed entirely in brown. He wore shiny brown shoes, a three piece suit, and a trilby hat, which was perched at a jaunty angle on the back of his head. A mop of thick, black curly hair was protruding from the front. He was reaching forward to light a cigarette for my mother. It was the first time I had ever seen her smoke. His hand was cupped across the cigarette protecting the flame of his lighter from the breeze. His long fingers were touching her cheek. I sensed trouble, I didn't like this stranger, but that was nothing unusual. I never liked anyone who got close to my mother, she belonged to me.

The pair of them sat smoking and talking for some time. There was a lot of laughter and Mum was giggling like a young girl. I had never heard her laugh like that before. Then, Mr. 'Brown' was on his way. He waved and shouted "Goodbye Michael." as he left, and headed off along the Horsefair towards Milk Street. I watched him walk away but I ignored him and I didn't reply.

"His name is Tom Burke," explained my mother when I questioned her. "He just wanted a chat."

That night was a cold one, and I was curled up against Mum's legs in front of the coal fire. She was trying to teach me to read, but I wasn't in the mood. Tommy Handley and ITMA were on the radio. I didn't understand a word of it, but loved to guffaw along with the studio audience. Looking back now, I can truly appreciate that magical combination of the coal fire, the flickering gaslights and the radio. It made for a very intimate and atmospheric experience, and the memories evoke very special feelings.

Suddenly, there was a tap on the front door.

"I'll go." Mum was quick off the mark, but I was quicker. This could be the German invasion, and I needed to get to Mrs. Grant first. I got to the door just before my mother.

"Hello Michael."

I blinked into the darkness. I knew the voice, and then I recognised him. It was Mr. Burke from the park

He was Irish; he spoke like Mrs. Grant, and he looked and sounded very much like Father Doyle. Father Doyle was the Catholic priest who called round to see us on a regular basis. I didn't like Father Doyle, and I didn't like Mr. Burke either. Mr. Burke smelt of beer and tobacco, he chain smoked, and he growled at my mother when she couldn't supply him with an ash tray.

I turned up the volume on the radio as Mum and Mr. Burke held a series of intense whispered conversations. I was irritated that his unexpected visit had caused me to miss the ending of ITMA, and now he was interfering with my enjoyment of Paul Temple. 'Paul Temple' was one of my favourite programmes, and I was engrossed in the current episode. Paul and his wife, Steve, were detectives and were close to solving yet another crime.

"By Timothy, look at this, Steve."

I loved the way that Paul Temple spoke, and the way that he always solved the crime. I had already decided that I would be a detective when I grew up, and I would say 'By Timothy.' I sometimes wondered if my father spoke like Paul Temple.

"I'll be after popping out to get some cigarettes. I won't be long." The door slammed behind Mr. Burke and he was gone. I was hoping he wouldn't return, but true to his word, he wasn't away for long.

"Tom will be staying with us for a couple of days." My mother broke the news as soon as the front door closed behind him. She looked nervous." Then, he will be going back to Ireland. He's got everything arranged."

She started to make up a bed on the sofa, using coats and cushions. I watched with a trace of smug satisfaction. The sofa looked far too small for Mr. Burke to relax, and he looked set to spend an uncomfortable night on it. I couldn't have been more wrong. Mr. Burke had the bed; I had the sofa. My night was a cold and restless one, but it wasn't long before I could hear Mr. Burke snoring contentedly. I missed the warmth and the comfort of my mother's body, and I lay there simmering with anger and resentment.

We were all up early the following morning, apart from the stranger. Mum seemed to sense my anger, and lifted me on to her knee. She shook me gently by the shoulders to get my attention, and then looked me directly in my eyes.

"Listen, this is very important." She shook me again, and then raised the index finger of her right hand to her lips.

"Shh! You mustn't say a word to anyone about anything." She glanced nervously over her shoulder in the direction of the bedroom, and lowered her voice. "Tom is a deserter from the Army." She shook me again. "If they find him, they will kill him." She ran her hand across her throat. Then she repeated the words slowly and clearly, "They will kill him; do you understand?"

I nodded. I didn't really understand, but I understood enough to know that my silence was important; I was also confident that their secret would be safe with me; wild horses wouldn't drag it from me.

I toddled across to see Mrs. Grant for breakfast. She had a slice of cake waiting for me, a very large slice. She hoisted up her substantial bosom and stood, arms folded and legs slightly apart, watching me eat. She suddenly moved closer, and she caught me off my guard, and went straight in for the kill.

"Did I see a man go into your house last night?"

I almost choked on my cake. Paul Temple had nothing on Mrs. Grant. I hadn't been expecting this. I prepared myself to tell a lie, but Mrs. Grant gave me no time to think. She went for the jugular.

"You wouldn't lie to me Michael would you? You're a good Catholic boy."

I chewed stoically, desperately playing for time, but Mrs. Grant was now wearing the look of a gambler who knows her sole remaining card is the ace of trumps. She lowered her face until our noses were almost touching.

"And I saw you open the door Michael."

I was done for. There was nowhere to run to, and no place to hide. I was not quite three, but was being forced into making the first big decision of my life. I made that decision. I decided that Mrs. Grant was my friend, and she was a friend who had to be trusted. I raised my right index finger to my lips, and lowered my voice to a whisper.

"Shh! You mustn't say anything to anyone. Tom is a deserter from the Army, and if they catch him, they will kill him." I ran my hand along my throat.

Mrs. Grant sat down very quickly. She sat motionless, breathing heavily and staring vacantly into space. She said nothing, but after a while, she waved me away and motioned me to leave. I walked home slowly; I figured I'd done quite well in difficult circumstances and I didn't say anything to Mum.

It was dark when the two Army Jeeps screeched to a halt outside the house. Eight soldiers, each wearing the distinctive red caps of the Military Police, clattered up the steps to our front door. They pushed my mother aside, and burst into the flat. Within seconds, they were dragging Mr. Burke down the stone corridor, helping him on his way with some firm blows from their truncheons. He was wearing a vest and long johns. He was begging for mercy and my mother was on her knees in the hallway; crying. The last soldier out was carrying Mr. Brown's clothes. He stopped, turned to my mother, and spat at her.

"You fucking whore!!" He spat again.

I threw myself at him and tried to punch him, but he held me at bay with a firm hand on my head.

I ran outside to watch them drive away. Mrs. Grant and several other neighbours were across the road, talking animatedly. Mrs. Grant moved away from the others, and beckoned me over to join her. I didn't go; I had this strong feeling, deep down inside, that my friend, Mrs. Grant, had betrayed me. I turned my back on her, and walked away. I knew that I was walking away from a friendship, and I was also walking away from a supply of sausage sandwiches, cakes and sweets. It was a difficult and painful decision, but I knew it was the correct one for me to make.

Mum cried nonstop for hours. She was still whimpering when the brick came crashing through the window. She stopped crying immediately, and. quietly and quickly she dressed me. Mary was still sleeping peacefully in the pushchair. Mum piled our bedding on top of her, and off we went into the black of the night. I was clutching the clock and my father's photo in one hand, and clinging on to Mum's coat with the other. I was tired and I was having tantrums long before we got to the top of Stokes Croft. I baulked completely when asked to climb Ninetree Hill, and Mum called on the services of a passing stranger, who scooped me up and carried me. I fell asleep in his arms almost immediately, still clinging on to the clock and my father's photo.

When I woke up in the morning, I was in a strange double bed, cuddling up to my mother, and we were living in a nice top floor flat in Kingsdown Parade. I learnt a lot that day, and I think I started the painful process of growing up.

One thing that I have discovered about going back in time, is that memory is an unreliable and shallow friend. There are no complete years, months, weeks, days or even hours. There are just a collection of scattered, random moments, which then fall into place like pieces of a jigsaw puzzle, to form a complete coherent picture. So it was with the few precious months we were to spend in Kingsdown Parade.

Without a shadow of doubt, we had moved onwards and upwards, and we were in a much better place; things were looking good for us, and everything about Kingsdown was an improvement on what had gone before. Our rooms in St Paul's had been small, damp, cramped, poorly lit, dirty and untidy. Now we had space, light, decent furniture, and rooms with a view. The house was enormous, and from the back bedroom I could see for miles. I sat for hours looking out, trying to work out where Germany was, and looking for my father.

We had also made our sudden and unexpected move from Badminton Road at that very special and magical time of the year when Mother Nature was working her annual miracles. Winter turned to spring, and then spring was transformed into summer. Overnight, or so it seemed, the grey skies and the relentless drizzling rain disappeared, and were replaced by blue skies and sunshine. The empty boughs on the trees were suddenly full of blossom, and then flowers. They were special times and for a brief period my life was filled with golden days.

"Depart from me ye cursed into everlasting fire, prepared for the devil and his angels." Father Doyle strode up and down the room, shouting, and waving his arms in the air. Mum fidgeted nervously with her handkerchief, and I watched and listened, wide eyed and open mouthed. This was better and scarier stuff than any of the ghost stories that my mother used to tell us as we huddled around the coal fire in the half light of Badminton Road. Mum could tell a good story, but Father Doyle's were even better.

It hadn't taken the Catholic priest very long to track us down for his weekly visit. My mother was keeping a promise that she had made to my father before he had gone away to war. She'd promised him that my sister and I would be brought up in the Catholic faith, and that she would, herself, convert to Catholicism.

"For I was hungry, and you gave me nothing to eat. I was thirsty, and you gave me nothing to drink."

He paused, smiled, and then sat next to my mother on the sofa. She looked edgy and uncomfortable.

I was studying the priest closely. He bore an uncanny resemblance to Mr. Burke, but unlike Mr. Burke, I was beginning to warm to him.

happily home, juggling with the piping hot bread, and I would always have the 'topper'. In the space of a just a few weeks, football and freshly baked bread had secured a place in my young heart.

Nothing good lasts forever. I was about to learn the same lesson for the second time. It was June 24th, and the day had started well. My mother had gone out on the previous night, and Peggy had been my baby sitter. I had proudly introduced her to my radio, to the Home Service, and to Paul Temple and his wife, Steve. She was clearly impressed, and we started off the following day with a game of 'Paul Temple' in the garden. We then moved upstairs, and Peggy suggested a game of 'Doctors and Nurses.' To my astonishment she undressed, and lay naked on the bed. I was too busy working out why the 'nurse' had undressed to notice anything other than her enormous feet. Oh for the innocence of childhood. I was enjoying the game when it was unfortunately interrupted by a piercing scream from downstairs. Peggy quickly slipped on her knickers and dress, took my hand and we rushed down.

The telegraph boy was standing awkwardly in the doorway. He was shifting uncomfortably from foot to foot. My mother was on her knees in the hallway, clutching a piece of paper. She screamed again and wailed, "What am I going to do? What am I going to do for money?"

Mrs. Woodruff was always good in a crisis and she took control. She spoke quietly to the boy at the door.

"I'm sorry, but there will be no tip." She directed him away and closed the door behind him.

She took the piece of paper from my mother's hand, studied it closely, and then read it aloud. 'Petty Officer Joseph Leo Kelly DK951937, missing in action, presumed killed.' She lifted me up, rocked me gently and then pressed my face to hers with a firm hand. She whispered in my ear.

"It's your father Michael. He's dead."

In war time, the arrival of a telegram invariably means bad news. Bad news always travels fast, and it wasn't long before the first callers arrived to offer their condolences and pay their respects. There was a lot of sobbing, kissing and hugging, and several of them pressed a coin into my hand. I felt no emotion; I was just numb and silent. Mrs. Woodruff suggested to Peggy that she took me out for a while, and armed with her sweet coupons and a two shilling piece, she led me up the road to Mrs. Tuck's shop in Cotham Road South. That shop was a treasure trove of sweets and chocolate. Shelf after shelf, all filled with jar upon jar of multi coloured goodies. I selected my favourites; the Sherbet Lemons.

"His father died today." Mrs. Tuck was meticulously weighing the sweets as Peggy made her dramatic announcement.

"He died in the war." She added as she received no response from Mrs. Tuck.

Mrs. Tuck grunted, and then rather grudgingly slipped an extra sweet into the bag.

"Thank you Mrs. Tuck." Peggy flashed her toothy smile, and then she took my hand. We laughed and chatted as we sauntered slowly down to Cotham Park.

There are the occasional days in your life which are sprinkled with magic. Special days you will always remember above all others. This was one such a day. It had started badly with the arrival of the telegram, but now it was looking up. Peggy and I sat on the grass, with the sun on our faces, and we sucked and crunched upon our Sherbet Lemons. We laughed aloud and pulled faces as the tart sourness of the sherbet exploded in our mouths. We held a competition to decide who could pull the funniest face. Peggy was the judge and I won every single game. We then played football and I beat her for the very first time.

The game over, I lay back, exhausted. I recall closing my eyes, and listening to the sound of the silence. I heard the humming and buzzing of the insects, the singing of the birds, and the distant sound of children at play. For what was probably the first time in my young life, I felt at peace with the world. I fell asleep, and I didn't dream.

Peggy woke me gently and told me it was time to go. She smoothed my hair and asked if was feeling alright, and then took my hand and led me slowly home. It was late afternoon when we arrived. I was feeling a vague sense of guilt. It didn't seem right that I had experienced happiness on a day when I should have been sad, but at the age of three, all emotions including guilt are fleeting and transitory. The day suddenly got even better, as my life turned full circle. We had left with the house in mourning; we arrived home to a different and happier place. There was a full scale party happening, and music was playing from Mrs. Woodruff's gramophone. A bottle of sherry was being shared with half a dozen neighbours. I stood in the doorway and saw Mrs. Woodruff's thin legs and enormous feet rushing towards me. For the second time that day she lifted me up, held me close, and whispered in my ear.

"It's your father Michael. He's alive."

The same Telegraph Boy had called again, but this time the telegram had contained better news. 'Lucky' Joe Kelly had survived the sinking of HMS Khartoum. The ship may have been sitting on the bed of the Red Sea, but Joe was safely on board HMS Kandahar, and was bound for Aden.

"He will be drunk tonight. I hope they have plenty of ice cold beer available." Mum was smiling again.

It was summertime, and every day seemed to bring sunshine. We feasted on fresh bread from Parker's, and fish and chips from Smith's shop at the far end of the road. Peggy and I played non-stop. We played 'Paul Temple', football, and 'Doctors and Nurses'. I was happy, I was sleeping well, and I had nightly dreams about Sherbet Lemons and Peggy's feet, but nothing good lasts forever.

It would have been early August. I was lying on my stomach supported by my elbows, with my head cupped in my hands. I was listening to ITMA.

"Can I do you now sir?" warbled Mrs. Mopp, the cleaning lady. The studio audience greeted her appearance, and the catch phrase with prolonged applause.

"Ah, there you are my little camp follower." retorted Tommy Handley. The audience roared with laughter again, and I joined in although I couldn't see the joke.

I turned around to see if my mother was laughing, and my heart stood still. She was standing in the open doorway, watching me. The pushchair was fully loaded, with the bedding piled high on top of my sleeping sister. Mum was silhouetted against the soft light from the hallway, and she looked like a film star. She was wearing a bottle green coat, with black fur trimming on the collar and the cuffs. The coat was pinched in at the waist showing off her figure, and her rich auburn hair cascaded over her shoulders. I thought for a brief moment that Mum was crying again, but I must have been mistaken, for she just swallowed hard, cleared her throat and smiled.

"We're moving." She mouthed the words silently.

Mum could get up quite a head of steam with that pushchair, and

I struggled to keep up with her as we raced along Kingsdown Parade. This time, I was clutching the clock, my photo, and my tennis ball. I was annoyed that I hadn't seen this coming. I hadn't noticed any warning signs. My inner 'Paul Temple' had switched off, taken his eye off the ball. He had grown soft and complacent with overindulgence on freshly baked bread, fish and chips, football, naked girls, large feet and Sherbet Lemons.

I felt like the Grand Old Duke of York. I had marched up to the top of the hill, and now I was marching back down again. We sped down Horfield Road and St Michael's Hill. We stormed up Perry Road and Park Row. We swept across Queens Road, and raced down Jacob's Well Road.

We stopped, eventually, in Hotwell Road, and Mum lit a cigarette in a doorway. It was a warm summer night. The moon was reflected on the river. I suddenly realised I hadn't said goodbye to Peggy, and I started to cry, just as my mother knocked on the door. It was only four months since the Mr. 'Brown' incident; I wasn't quite ready for another new life.

2 WOMEN AND CHILDREN FIRST

I liked our new house. We looked down on to the river, and HMS Flying Fox was berthed right under our living room window. Our new landlord was Mr. Lloyd. He was a big man with an even bigger voice. He had thick white hair, swept back, without a parting, and bushy white eyebrows. His wife, Meryl, also had white hair and even bushier eyebrows, but she was quieter than Mr. Lloyd

"She's 'Chapel', he's 'spit and sawdust'", said Mum.

There were two other families in the house, the Edwards, and the Williams, but Mr. Lloyd was in charge. He was one of the many 'Little Hitlers' that we spawned during the war years.

"He's a noisy bleeder; a natural leader." My mother had a way with words. "He's Welsh, probably from Newport." She added, as if by way of explanation. I would, in time, understand the venom that I detected in her voice when she spoke those words.

Although not a member of any official organization, Mr. Lloyd dressed in a navy blue siren suit, similar to the ones worn by Winston Churchill, and wore a metal helmet with a strap around his chin. A large silver whistle was secured around his neck by a white ribbon.

Mr. Lloyd held numerous air raid drills, to which we were summoned by a shrill blast of his whistle. We would line up in front of the Anderson Air Raid Shelter in the tiny back garden.

"We approach the shelter in a calm and orderly fashion." I had learnt the lecture off by heart and Mum would always giggle as I mouthed the words behind his back.

"There is one sacred and unbreakable rule." His voice rose to a lilting crescendo. "All women and children go first." He bowed, and extended his left hand, palm upwards in the direction of the shelter.

"So it's Mrs. Kelly and child." He waved Mum, who was carrying my sister, towards the entrance, with an exaggerated sweep of his right hand.

"We have Master Kelly next." I had the same treatment, and then I was followed by the three wives.

"Mr. Edwards, Mr. Williams and I will be engaged on other much more important duties; like fire-fighting and rescues."

I didn't like it much in the Anderson Shelter. It was damp, dark and smelly, but fortunately we never remained in there for any long period of time. Mum said all the drills and practices were 'rubbish'.

I did enjoy having male company in the house and having the three male role models. I followed Mr. Lloyd around everywhere like a little shadow, and he allowed me to join the three of them around the kitchen table for morning tea. I would drink, like them, from a large, chipped enamel mug. Like them, I would wipe my mouth with the back of my hand. I even tried to belch like them, but I couldn't master the belch. My vocabulary was growing, however. Mr. Lloyd was the first man I knew in my life, who suffered from Tourette's syndrome. He was incapable of completing any sentence without including a long string of expletives.

"Jerry won't come over by here," he would say. "We are bloody bristling with bloody barrage balloons and bloody guns." Then, in very explicit detail he would describe Jerry's potential fate. We would all listen, nod in agreement, slurp our tea, wipe our mouths with the back of our hands, and then the other three would belch.

We were getting sporadic air raids now, and the sirens would frequently wail their alarms. On September 25th the siren sounded for the 151st time. Many of the warnings had been false alarms and by now people were beginning to ignore the sirens. This time, however, the warning was real. 168 bombs were dropped in 45 seconds. The target was the Bristol Aeroplane Works at Filton in the north of the city. Ninety one people working at the factory were killed. Another 69 people living in the area were also killed. Nine hundred houses were damaged. There was no anti-aircraft fire or fighter aircraft to cover the factory. Two days later, on September 27th, the Luftwaffe tried another raid on the Bristol Aeroplane Works. This time a squadron of RAF Hurricane fighter planes was there to meet them. After a 'dog fight' over the city, which brought many people out of their houses to watch, the German planes flew away without reaching their target.

When the sirens sounded at 6.22 pm on Sunday November 24th, it was the 338th alert of the war. Mr. Lloyd blew his whistle, and we all straggled slowly out of the house and into the garden. We came somewhat reluctantly and complainingly, but without fear. It had been a typical lazy November Sunday. There had been bread and jam for tea, with real butter instead of margarine. That was our Sunday treat.

"We approach the shelter in a calm and orderly manner." Mr. Lloyd rubbed his hands in anticipation as he started his usual speech.

"There is one sacred, unbreakable rule..." His voiced tailed away. Suddenly, the air was heavy with the drone of German bombers. The searchlights frantically scanned the skies, the anti-aircraft guns clattered into action.

I stood fascinated and fearless because I knew exactly what to expect; I knew what was coming. Mr. Lloyd had told us so many times and explained it all very clearly at the breakfast table.

"Jerry won't come over by here. We are bloody bristling with bloody barrage balloons and bloody guns. Jerry knows we will just blow the fuckers out of the fucking sky."

Within moments, everything had changed. One minute there was complete darkness, the next, the city was illuminated by the falling parachute flares.

I stood there, holding Mum's hand and waited for 'Jerry' to come falling out of the sky. Instead, the first high explosive bomb fell. It sounded close, and Mr. Lloyd's confidence disappeared in a flash.

"Fuck me!" He stood motionless, seemingly transfixed to the spot.

Two more bombs fell in quick succession.

"Don't just stand there, get in the bloody shelter." Mrs. Lloyd took control.

I don't know what happened to the 'One sacred, unbreakable rule', the 'Women and children first', but the next thing I saw was Mr. Lloyd disappearing into the shelter. He was quickly followed by Mr. Williams and Mr. Edwards. The three wives then dived in, Mrs. Lloyd was last. She only just fitted through the narrow opening. She left me with a mental picture of skirts, petticoats, stockings, suspenders, knickers and cellulite. The door snapped shut.

Another bomb fell and my mother gave a little scream, and jumped like a startled rabbit.

"Get in the bloody house under the bloody stairs." Mr. Lloyd's muffled voice shouted. He was back in charge.

I only wish my vocabulary was wide enough to adequately describe the terror of that night, as we sat in total darkness, and it rained bombs on Bristol. My sister slept, and my mother drew her knees up to her chest, covered her ears with her hands and rocked slowly backwards and forwards. She started singing; quietly at first, but then louder as the bombing increased in intensity. She sang the same song over and over again. She sang for six hours. She sang her favourite song of the moment.

The other night dear, as I lay sleeping
I dreamt I held you in my arms
But when I awoke, dear, I was mistaken
So I hung my head and I cried

You are my sunshine, my only sunshine
You make me happy when skies are grey
You'll never know dear, how much I love you
Please don't take my sunshine away

I'll always love you and make you happy
If you will only say the same
But if you leave me and love another
You'll regret it all someday:

You are my sunshine, my only sunshine
You make me happy when skies are grey
You'll never know dear, how much I love you
Please don't take my sunshine away

You told me once, dear, you really loved me
And no one else could come between
But now you've left me and love another;
You have shattered all of my dreams:

You are my sunshine, my only sunshine
You make me happy when skies are grey
You'll never know dear, how much I love you
Please don't take my sunshine away

I closed my eyes, and I tried to block out the sound of the bombs. Eventually, I found a way. I took myself back in time to Ashley Road. I was marching again with the Salvation Army Band. I was struggling to stay in step, but the big, fat bass drummer was looking down at me, smiling and winking. I had my very own big bass drum, and he nodded approvingly as together we beat our drums in perfect unison. We beat them very loudly and we beat them in perfect time with each exploding bomb. Boom! Boom! Boom! Boom!

We marched and played until the final bombs had fallen, and the 'Raiders passed' siren sounded. We crawled out of the cupboard in the early hours of the morning. Mr. Lloyd and his clan were noisily drinking tea, and eating toast in the kitchen.

"You were the fucking lucky ones in there. Doubt that you gave us a single thought. It was fucking hell in that shelter." He wiped his mouth with the back of his hand, and belched.

I decided that when I grew up, I would become a German pilot, and I would drop bombs on Mr. Lloyd every night of the week.

135 German bombers, flying in perfect formation, had crossed the channel that night to deliver their deadly cargo of bombs on the city. Our much vaunted defences had proved to be wholly inadequate, and for six hours, virtually unopposed, the planes spewed their incendiary and high explosive bombs into the heart of the city. 10,000 homes were damaged, factories, churches and shops destroyed. 207 killed, 187 seriously injured, 703 slightly injured. Much of our architectural heritage had vanished overnight. Bristol had been damaged beyond repair, and would never be the same again.

"Jerry won't be coming over by here anymore." Mr. Lloyd had returned from his 'fact finding' visit to the city centre. He was still wearing his navy blue tunic and steel helmet. I waited for the usual stream of expletives, and he didn't disappoint.

"There's fuck all left to bomb; it's all fucking gone. It's all blown to smithereens." He chuckled to himself. His arrogance and self-confidence seemed to have returned. "That's unless you want to shop at the fucking Co-op in Castle Street. That's still standing."

We were sitting around the kitchen table, and we all chuckled along with him. We slurped our hot, sweet tea from our chipped enamel mugs, wiped our mouths with the backs of our hands, and I managed to produce my maiden belch. It all felt good; I now considered myself a man.

"So if that's how Jerry wants to play it lads, let's show him what we can do. Just remember, all's fair in love and war." Mr. Lloyd stretched his arms in the air, and yawned. "It's every man for himself now boyos. I'm off; I'm going to catch up on some sleep."

The maiden belch had put a spring back into my step, and I had a little swagger as I went upstairs to join Mum. I told her what Mr. Lloyd had said about his 'fact finding' visit. She looked concerned.

"I need to pop out myself." she said quietly. "Can you look after Mary?"

Mary was almost two now, and was just beginning to take an interest in life. She was crawling, and almost speaking. I even tried to have a chat with her about the war, but she didn't appear to understand me. When Mum returned, she looked upbeat, cheerful, and very excited.

"We've got a place in the tunnel." she proudly announced. "We will be safe now. They won't get us in there."

She was wearing her 'Hedy Lamarr' face.

Whenever she was pleased or excited, Mum always wore, what I called, her 'Hedy Lamarr' face.

Hedy Lamarr was a famous film star in the 1940s, and my mother bore a remarkable resemblance to her. Almost on a daily basis, completely random strangers would comment on it. Mum would always pretend to be disinterested, but as soon as we got home, out would come the mirror, and she would study her reflection for ages, and from all angles. She was, by her own admission, both vain and very insecure. As she studied her image, her nostrils would flare, and her lips would tighten .The flared nostrils and the tight lipped smile produced her 'Hedy Lamarr' look.

I just sat and waited patiently for the inevitable question.

"Do I really look like Hedy Lamarr?"

I would nod and smile back. I didn't have a clue really, but I knew it made her happy, and I liked it when Mum was happy.

"Mea culpa, Mea culpa, Mea maxima culpa." Father Doyle was at it again. He stood there beating his chest with his right fist, and telling us another story. Not only could he tell a good story, but he could tell them in different languages.

"It's Latin." Mum explained. "All Roman Catholics speak Latin."

Mum and I were kneeling on the bare floorboards, and the priest was blessing us, and teaching us how to pray. Our hands were folded together, and our heads were bowed. Our eyes should have been closed, but I was cheating, and peeping out of the corner of my right eye.

Father Doyle sprinkled us with water. It wasn't ordinary water; it was holy water.

"In nomine Patris Et Filii Et Spiritus Sancti." I watched as Father Doyle placed his hand on my mother's head. He moved closer and Mum edged away from him. She then stood up quickly, and dragged me to my feet at the same time.

"I must prepare Michael for the tunnel now. Thank you Father. That was all very interesting."

Father Doyle was bent almost double as he shuffled away and out of the room. I heard him grumbling under his breath as he clumped off down the stairs.

Despite Mr. Lloyd's assertions that 'Jerry' wouldn't be back, Mum was taking no chances.

"We have a place in the tunnel. We will be safe now."

'The tunnel', was a 525 feet stretch that ran under Bridge Valley Road. It was part of the defunct Port and Pier Railway. Our 'place' was deep in the bowels of the Avon Gorge, at the rear of the tunnel. When we arrived on that first night, there were thousands clamouring to get in. The man on the door was very friendly, and waved us through with a smile, a nod, and a wink. As we entered, I spotted him patting my mother on her bum. I thought she might get angry with him, but she smiled, and her nostrils flared. I decided that the man must have told her that she looked like Hedy Lamarr.

Inside, that tunnel was not a very pleasant place. It was dark, damp and very, very smelly. An official report into the tunnel stated: 'it deserved full marks for possessing everything that a shelter should not possess'.

The smell started as soon as you entered and became progressively worse as you made your way along. It was the first time I had witnessed our class structure in operation. The better off had their positions nearest the entrance, the middle classes were halfway up, and we peasants were at the back, where the stench was almost unbearable.

Another official report stated:

'A little over half way along, there is another brick wall. Beyond this the walls are whitewashed and bunks four across have been built. The poorest and dirtiest people of them all are using this end. The children are four to a bunk. Lighting is by candles and oil lamps. There is a brick wall with sackcloth; on the other side are closets labelled M and W. The closets are never empty for more than 30 seconds at a time; they serve over a thousand people. There is a stinking tang of chlorine.'

The German bombers came back in force on the night of December 2. The raid started at 16 minutes past 6 and lasted until 11 o'clock. 156 people killed, 149 seriously injured and 121 slightly injured. Redfield, Cotham, Redland, St Michael's Hill, Welsh Back, Nelson Street, Portland Square, St Paul's, Bridewell and Wills' No. 1 factory were among the damaged areas. We heard the bombing, but only as dull, distant thuds. The Portway tunnel may have been a hell hole, but to our little 'poor and dirty' family, it was paradise.

We trudged home at midnight. I was sneezing, coughing and wheezing. Mary was sleeping, and Mum had a steely glint in her green eyes.

"They won't get us whilst we are in there Michael. We will be as safe as houses." She stooped and kissed me on my head.

"Mr. Lloyd can stick his Anderson shelter where the sun doesn't shine."

We never got much sleep in the tunnel during the blitz, but we slept at home whenever we could. This enabled me to get very close to my mother. We would lie in the bed together at every available opportunity, and she would tell me stories about her childhood. She told me stories about her early life in Long Ashton, the tiny village just outside Bristol. How she had been the youngest of 10 children, and had enjoyed an ideal childhood until her mother, and two of her favourite brothers had died of Tuberculosis.

"I could never go through that again." She sobbed as she described their deaths.

Her father had remarried, but she described her step mother as cruel and heartless.

"She wanted me out, and Dad wasn't strong enough to fight her."

Mum left home eventually and had gone into service at Ashton Court Mansion.

"I did well." she said proudly. "I was 'Silver Service'."

She had fallen in love with Fred Mears, the head gardener at the Estate, and she described how Fred would take her to Weston super Mare in the side car of his motor cycle. He took her there at every opportunity, and they'd lie together in the sand dunes. She said they'd made love as the sun set over the Channel. She started crying again as she told me how she had become pregnant; how Fred had vowed his undying love and support. Just a few weeks later he'd left on what Mum described as 'the fastest motorbike in the west'. He was heading for home.

"He was Welsh, from Newport," Mum chuckled. "Just like Mr. Lloyd."

The baby, Ivan, had been placed into care. Mum didn't know what had happened to him, or where he was.

We lived like cavemen for the duration of the Bristol blitz, spending more time in the tunnel than in our own home. The winter of 1940/1 was bitterly cold, and the bombers returned again and again. I watched my mother, suffering from a lack of sleep. I watched her as she counted the pennies, and struggled to feed us, and to keep us warm. I was suffering badly myself from repeated colds and coughs.

We were close to breaking point, and on the night of April 11th, we finally cracked. It was the night of the 'Good Friday raid'.

The raid on March 16 had been the worst so far. 257 killed and 391 injured, as the German bombers dropped 800 high-explosive and several thousand incendiary bombs on the city. The bombing started at around 8.30 p.m., and lasted until 4.12 a.m. Whitehall, Eastville and Fishponds bore the brunt of the first phase, and Easton, St Paul's and Kingsdown were also badly affected.

The Germans came again on March 20th, 1941.

Mum was mumbling and grumbling as she rubbed the Wintergreen ointment on my bare chest.

"For God's sake Michael," she snapped, "I feel as if it's one bloody thing after another."

I couldn't see that it was my fault, but I sort of understood her. It really did feel as if every brand new day brought with it a fresh problem. One after another for which my mother had to find a solution.

Today, it was my health that was the cause for concern. I had always been a chesty child, and already had two bouts of pneumonia chalked up on my medical records. Now, all those hours in that damp, dark, cold tunnel had taken their toll, and I was a wheezing, sneezing wreck. I was struggling to breathe, and running a high temperature. I badly needed a doctor, but this was 1941, and the National Health Service was still a distant dream. A doctor's visit cost money; real money, and as Mum would frequently point out, ' Money didn't live in our house.'

Mum's engagement ring, with its sparkling blue and white stones, had bailed us out of several crises already. In truth, it had probably spent more time in the pawn shop than out of it, but her wedding ring had always remained firmly glued to her finger. Now, she sat looking pensively out of the window, staring across the river, lost in thought. She twisted and turned the ring, first one way, and then the other. Finally, with a deep sigh and a sad face, it came off. She kissed it, wrapped it in newspaper, and away it went to Mr. Keeler's pawn shop.

As it turned out, she could have spared herself all the anxiety and the trauma, because the doctor, when he finally arrived, took one look at our room and at me, and then waved away all of Mum's offers of payment.

He was a tall, somewhat bulky man, with thick, dark, wavy hair, a purple nose and a face like a benevolent bloodhound. It was a nice face though, with laughing eyes, a kind smile and a soft, gentle voice. He was wearing a pale blue, open necked shirt, and a light grey jacket, with dark blue leather patches on each elbow. Mum had always taught me that you could tell a man's position in society, by the number of pens that he carried in his breast pocket. The doctor's pocket was simply bristling with pens, pencils and gold and silver instruments. I decided that in terms of importance, he was right up there with King George, Winston Churchill, Mr. Hitler, Mr. Lloyd and the man named Ted, who wore a white coat, and ran the pig's trotter and chitterlings shop, which was tucked away behind the

Hippodrome, in Denmark Street.

The doctor opened up his shiny black bag and peeled on a pair of surgical gloves. He whistled tunelessly through his teeth as he took my temperature and checked my pulse, and then fell silent, listening intently, as he poked me with the cold stethoscope. Satisfied, he took a large, red leather bound book from the bag, and scribbled his notes. I noticed that he was using red ink.

"Pneumonia, Mrs. Kelly," he spoke without looking up or interrupting the writing. "But I think that you knew that already."

He expertly placed a piece of blotting paper inside the book, closed it and looked up.

"That makes three attacks now. That is far too many for young lungs to cope with. The child needs rest, warmth, and above all else..." he hesitated and sighed. "Keep away from that confounded tunnel. Another night in there could kill him."

We all get times in our lives, sadly infrequent, when we just get lucky. I guess that this was our turn; it was our time. The German bombers stayed away for night, after night, after night. I was allowed to heal in my own time, in my own bed, and in my own home.

It was April 9th, 1941, and it was almost Easter. I had almost fully recovered and Mum told me about Easter biscuits. She told me about their texture, their taste, the spices, the currants and the sugar. She made a circle using the middle fingers and thumbs of both hands to demonstrate their size. I almost passed out with excitement when she promised to get some for Good Friday.

It came as quite a shock when the sirens wailed their warning just before 10pm. I leaped out of bed, not sure what was going to happen.

'Another night in there could kill him.' I had remembered the doctor's words, and I suspect that Mum had as well.

She walked calmly to the window, peeped through the blackout curtains, and signaled me to return to bed.

"No tunnel tonight," she smiled, "it's only a small raid."

She took my father's photo from behind the clock on the shelf, and we all cuddled up in bed together.

Mum was in the middle, with a pillow supporting her back as she sat with her knees tucked up. I lay with my head on her shoulder, and my arm around her waist. Mary was asleep, as usual, contentedly sucking her thumb. Mum had never spoken much about Dad, but now, with the photo just visible in the light of the flickering candle, she told me the story about him. She told me how they had met at the foot of the Cabot Tower on Brandon Hill. She described how they had lain on the grass and how they had made me, and then married.

"He is a good man." she smiled to herself, "Unless he has the drink in him." she added in a whisper.

We lay in silence for a short while, and then she told me a very sad story.

She told me how, long before he had known Mum, my father had met, fallen in love with, and then married a young girl in Weymouth. Her name was Lilian. They had a child, a boy named Dennis. Lilian had died shortly after childbirth.

Mum didn't speak for a while, and when she started talking again, she was wearing her 'crying' voice.

"Your father loved her more than he will ever love me." she whispered sadly. "But you and Mary were the happy ending to the story," she tousled my hair, "he worships the pair of you."

The bombing was sporadic and slowly died away. We cuddled up and fell asleep. I had a dream about Easter biscuits.

April 10th 1941, and I rose early in the morning; awoken by the sound of Mr. Lloyd's booming voice and the clanking of the mugs in the kitchen below. I had missed the interaction with the men of the house during my illness, and I now crept downstairs to join them. I was worried that Mr. Lloyd might have forgotten me, but my fears were groundless. He greeted me like an old friend.

"Look what the fucking wind has blown in." he banged his mug down on the table. "It's fucking Lazarus!!"

They all burst out laughing, and I joined in, although I didn't understand the joke.

Mr. Lloyd then made me my 'usual', a half mug of hot, sweet, very milky tea, and I sat down in my chair.

We all sat slurping and burping, all waiting for Mr. Lloyd's report on the previous night's bombing. We didn't have to wait long.

"Avonmouth copped a packet." he wiped his mouth with the back of his hand, "and we copped three big bastards in Broadmead, and Newfoundland Road." He made the sign of the cross, just like Father

Doyle did. I copied him, like Father Doyle had taught me. They all laughed, but I didn't join in.

Mr. Lloyd stretched and yawned. "All's fair in love and war; it's every man for himself."

I knew that the breakfast meeting was over, and trudged back upstairs to remind Mum about the Easter biscuits.

April 11th 1941

It was Good Friday, and Mum went shopping. She came back with some Easter biscuits. We could only afford two, so Mum and Mary had to share one. The biscuit was delicious, and it was my lucky day, because Mum wasn't very hungry, and she gave me most of her half.

Father Doyle called in the afternoon. Mum told me to act as if I were still ill. She sat at the top of the bed with me, and told Father Doyle he should keep his distance, as what I had was very infectious. He stood by the door and told us a story about Easter.

He told us about the Last Supper and Judas Iscariot. He told us about Pontius Pilate and Barabbas, and then he told us about Jesus Christ. How he was forced to wear a crown of thorns, and how he carried the heavy cross up the hill of Mount Calvary. He told us how Jesus was crucified and died. It was a cracking story and I was right into it. I was waiting anxiously for the happy ending, and I was quite disappointed when Mum interrupted to tell Father Doyle that it was time for him to leave. He threw some holy water at me from the bottom of the bed, shouted 'Dominus vobiscum', and made a hasty exit down the wooden stairs.

Back then, when our city was under nightly siege from the German bombers, I would always go to bed fully clothed, apart from my boots, which sat by the side of the bed. That way, we were always ready for a quick getaway. I often wondered if my mother ever slept. She always seemed to be there at the ready when the sirens sounded. She roused me from a deep sleep at just before nine o'clock that night. We sat and listened to Alvar Lidell reading the nine o'clock news. Yet again, there was no good news. Our armies were in retreat, our shipping was being sunk and our cities bombed. I waited in vain for my father to get a mention, but once again, he didn't.

"I don't know why we bother to listen." Mum looked glum. She took off my shirt, lifted my vest and started to rub the Wintergreen on my chest. I was still half asleep and not really listening as she chatted away.

Just before ten o'clock, the sirens sounded for the 538th time since war had been declared. This time, it was the real thing. The guns were barking away, the searchlights were scanning the skies like demented fire flies, and the dreaded drone of the bombers filled the air. Mum sat on the bottom of the bed, with her head in her hands. She started to cry as she rocked back and forth.

"I don't know what to do" she said helplessly.

I was listening to the voices in my head. They were doing battle. It was Mr. Lloyd versus the Doctor

'Another night in there could kill him.'

'If one of those big bastards has got your name on it, you're a goner.'

'It's every man for himself.'

I knew what I had to do.

Mr. Lloyd won the day; I jumped off the bed, and sprinted out of the house. I was heading for the sanctuary of my tunnel. I heard Mum's frantic voice calling me. Slowly, it faded into the distance, as I ran bare-footed and bare-chested down Hotwell Road.

Mr. Lloyd had been adamant. There was no chance of 'Jerry' coming to call on Good Friday. 'Stands to bloody reason.' he said. 'Jerry' didn't come over at Christmas, so he won't be over for bloody Easter.' Yet again, Mr. Lloyd was wrong.

It was quite a long haul from where we lived in Hotwell Road to the tunnel on the Portway. I had made the journey on many occasions with my mother, but never in the middle of a major air raid. I had always walked slowly; lagging behind Mum; usually dragging my heels, and insisting on numerous pit stops along the way. That Good Friday night was very different. By the time I had set out on my panic fuelled dash to safety, the raid was in full swing. The first wave of enemy bombers had avoided the customary frenzied, but wholly ineffective gun fire, and the first bombs had been delivered. Amongst the early casualties were the buildings housing the Cheltenham Road Library, and the neighbouring Colston's Girls'

School.

I was still only three, and my running style was, to say the least, lacking in coordination. My arms and legs had minds of their own, and flapped wildly in different directions, but I had no intention of hanging around, and the one hundred and fifty three German bombers flying overhead in perfect formation added both strength and resolve to my young limbs. Furthermore, the knowledge that any one of the planes could also be carrying the 'big bastard with my name written on it', gave wings to my heels. That night, I ran every single step of the way, and to my eternal shame, I ran with neither a backward glance, nor a second thought for the safety and welfare of the mother and sister whom I had left behind.

The man on the door of the tunnel looked quite startled as I burst past him, and splashed my barefooted path through the puddles. I was heading towards my bunk at the very far end of the tunnel. A queue was already forming for the smelly toilet block behind my bunk, and the crowd gave me a good natured round of applause as I arrived.

I knew Mr. Brookes would be waiting; he always was. He was sitting, as usual, on his bunk. He was peering anxiously into the gloom, and looking out for Mum. Mr. Brookes slept on the lower bunk, which was directly underneath me. He was a good looking man, with dark hair, a black moustache, and a shiny white, sparkling smile. He bore a striking resemblance to Clark Gable, the famous film star, but he had a high pitched squeaky voice. He sounded just like Donald Duck, and to make matters worse, he was afflicted with a very bad stutter.

I liked Mr. Brookes. He always made me laugh, and he always made Mum smile. He was one of those people who constantly told her she looked like Hedy Lamarr. More importantly, he always had a large bag of toffees in his pocket, and I loved toffees. I loved them more than anything in the world, apart from Easter biscuits, or maybe fish and chips, and maybe pig's trotters.

"Where's your m-m-m-m-mother?" enquired Mr. Brookes as he clasped his hands together and gave me a leg up to the upper bunk. His stutter always seemed to be far worse whenever Mum was involved. I waved vaguely in the direction of the entrance. I never dared to speak with Mr. Brookes myself. On the one occasion I had, I found myself mimicking his stutter, so I restricted myself to sign language only.

We didn't have long to wait. Mum wasn't far behind me, and she soon came splashing through the puddles herself. She was carrying Mary in one arm, and my shirt, a pullover, my boots, a pair of socks and a dry blanket in the other. Her face was a mixture of relief and anger. I knew that look well, and experience told me the anger would prevail. I prepared myself for a smack. It never arrived, because Mr. Brookes stood between us with his arms outstretched.

"L-L-Leave it be, M-M-M-Mrs. Kelly. He's only a y-y-young child. We are fighting the b-b-b-b-bloody Germans, not each other."

Mum let it be, and Mr. Brookes gave me a toffee. Mum dressed me, and tucked me in for the night.

I always tried to sleep, but sleep was hard to come by in the tunnel. The canvas in my bunk was damp and rotting, there were more holes than canvas, and I was basically lying on the rubber webbing, and could clearly see Mr. Brookes in his bunk below me. There was a constant buzz of nervous conversations. The toilet queue shuffled in, and back out again. Mothers scolded their children, and the children cried. Men drank beer, played cards, and argued, with the arguments becoming louder as the drinking increased. The little, old, white haired man who lounged in his brightly coloured deck chair would, from time to time, squeeze a tune from his accordion, and Mr. Brookes would squeak and stutter away, as he chatted nonstop with my mother. Mum sat, always looking extremely uncomfortable, in a wooden dining chair, cradling Mary in her arms. Mr. Brookes alternated between sitting and lying on his bunk.

The only light in the tunnel came from the handful of oil lamps and candles people had brought with them. These provided an eerie, yellowish half-light, and created strange, flickering shadows on the brick walls. Water ran down the walls, and dripped constantly from the curved roof.

The early bombing was light and sounded to be far away. We felt in no immediate danger, and it came as no surprise when the all clear sounded before midnight. Mum rapidly prepared us for our homeward journey. I could clearly hear the disappointment in Mr. Brookes' squeak as he said his goodbyes, and gave me another toffee. We lingered on the way out, and Mum had a chat, and shared a cigarette with the man on the door. I was glad that she did, because within minutes, and before we had left, the sirens wailed the alarm again. The Luftwaffe had regrouped and they were back for another go. This time it felt and sounded as if they meant business. The bombs sounded closer. It felt as if we were the target, and we were all uneasy.

Somehow, I managed to get to sleep, but it was a troubled sleep, and a troubled sleep meant troubled dreams. I dreamt that I was helping Jesus Christ carry his cross up the slopes of Mount Calvary. Jesus was wearing his crown of thorns, and the blood was streaming down his face. The cross was over his shoulders, and I was doing my best to lift it from the base. It was too heavy for me, and I wasn't much of a help, but I struggled on, doing my best. Mr. Lloyd was with us, and he was waving his fists, and swearing at the Roman soldiers. Father Doyle was beating his chest and shouting 'Pax vobiscum.' I suddenly realised I was bursting for a pee. There was a low stone wall to our left, and I asked Jesus for permission to go behind it to relieve myself. He nodded agreement, and as he nodded, the blood on his face splattered on to mine. I went behind the wall, and emptied what was a very full bladder. When I came back, the road was empty. Everyone had gone. It started to rain heavily, and I raised my face to the skies. The rain washed away the blood of Christ, but then I heard shouting. I woke up just as another drip from the ceiling of the tunnel landed on my face.

I realised I had been dreaming, and then I realised I had wet myself; I had wet my bunk, and I had wet Mr. Brookes. He was on his feet now, a look of disgust on his face as he shouted at Mum whilst he wiped himself down with the backs of his fingers.

"He's just a child." said Mum defensively.

"He's b-b-b-bloody three." Mr. Brookes squeaked loudly in reply.

I needed to put him straight. I leant over the side of my bunk and looked him in the eyes.

"I'm not b-b-b-bloody three." I yelled. I'm nearly f-f-f-four."

There was a stunned silence, and then slowly, everyone started to laugh. Even Mr. Brookes joined in and the old man in the deck chair squeezed his accordion, and played a tune. Everyone joined in and sang along with a rousing chorus of K-K-K-Katie, b-b-beautiful Katie,

You're the only g-g-g-girl that I adore.

I felt a warm glow of satisfaction. It felt as if I had just told my first adult joke.

The 'all clear' sounded at four thirty and as everyone else settled down to sleep, we prepared to make our way home. Mum had a brief chat with the man on the door, and then we set off.

I will never forget the walk home that night. It's just as if some great artist had painted a canvas, and placed it inside my head. The moon smiled down at its reflection on the river, and we had what was almost the perfect silence. It was broken only by the sound of our footsteps. Mum was wearing the same green coat, with the black fur trim; the same coat she had worn when we'd made our journey from Kingsdown to Hotwells all those months earlier. Mary, who was dressed all in pink, was leaning over Mum's left shoulder, and she was oblivious to everything. She was chuckling and chatting away to the white woolen doll which Mum had knitted for her. I was waddling along in the rear; lagging behind with my trousers wet, cold and clammy against my thighs. My socks were down around my ankles, and the early morning breeze was whipping cold against my bare legs. All I wanted was some sleep and some food.

We turned the final bend into our bit of Hotwell Road, and walked into an inferno. Anchor Road was burning from one end to the other. Jacob's Wells Road was badly damaged, and there was a massive fire on College Green as the big shop that Mum loved so much became a pile of smouldering embers, and a memory. The sky over Brandon Hill was blood red, and Park Row was on fire yet again.

A neighbour came running down the road, threw her arms around my mother, and whispered something in her ear. The pair of them sobbed together, as they rocked in one another's arms for several minutes. Every window in our house, together with most of the doors had disappeared. We spent the night in a strange bed, in a strange house, and when I woke up, it was late afternoon. Mum was dressed, ready and waiting.

"We're moving." She whispered. This time I didn't argue. This time I didn't mind. This time I wanted to go.

Mum had already rescued the clock, Dad's photo and my tennis ball, so we set off down the road. We were heading off to another adventure. Mary was leaning over Mum's shoulder again, still playing with her doll, still chuckling and chatting. Mum expertly steered the push chair with her spare hand.

"It will be a new life and a better life." Mum smiled and strode off at speed again. "We're going to Long Ashton; we're going home."

I asked to see Mr. Lloyd. I wanted to say goodbye. But my request only started Mum crying again. She explained that he was still in town, doing a 'fact find'. I wanted to believe her, but I had seen the hole in the garden where the Anderson shelter had once stood, and I was worried.

I slowly fell behind, but I wasn't dragging my heels. In fact, there was just a hint of a swagger in my step. I'd realised that it was Saturday, and on a Saturday we always had cheese and chips for supper. That was one of my most favourite things in the whole world. All I wanted now was for Mum to stop crying.

3 IN SICKNESS AND IN HEALTH

We didn't know it as we set out on our journey to Long Ashton, but that Good Friday raid was to be the last of the major raids carried out over Bristol. The German Luftwaffe next turned their attentions to Belfast, London, Portsmouth, Plymouth, Sunderland and then to the East, and the Russian front. There would be a few more small, but damaging raids on our city, but the siege of Bristol was all but over.

I didn't know what lay ahead of us as we marched off down Hotwell Road on that spring afternoon back in April 1941. Mum had spoken about a new and a better life, and what Mum promised, she usually delivered. I was feeling quite excited about the prospect of living in the country, but I wasn't looking forward to the journey. Mum had warned me it was a long walk to Long Ashton, and had told me to conserve my energy. I was doing just that, and walking with exaggerated slowness as I followed her and the pushchair down the road. We had only travelled but a few hundred yards, and I was already beginning to fall behind. Mum stopped as we approached Ambra Vale, and beckoned for me to catch up. She was in the middle of lecturing me when I spotted him. He was sitting on a wall on the corner; just smiling, smoking and watching us. It felt almost as if he had been waiting for us. It was the man from the door at the tunnel.

He gave Mum a cigarette, and they smoked, chatted and laughed for quite some time. I heard him telling Mum that Mr. Churchill had visited Bristol earlier that day, and he described how the crowd had booed the great man. He also told her that the Council had been trying to close the tunnel. I was engrossed, and fascinated. He was just as good at 'fact finding' as Mr. Lloyd had been. I heard Mum call him 'Jacob'. Now I knew his name.

He had even worse news to tell us. A single bomb had destroyed St Philips Bridge and had taken out the electrical supply for the Tramway Service.

"I doubt that there will be any more trams until the war is over." He looked quite sad, and I felt very sad. I always enjoyed riding on the trams. I liked the noise and the way that they swung around the corners.

Jacob appeared to be in a hurry. He inhaled deeply on his cigarette, and then threw the end away. He sighed deeply and peered at his watch.

"We'd better get moving. It's getting late."

He reached down, placed his hands underneath my armpits and lifted me up to face level. He was very strong. I felt quite safe as he held me aloft and looked me directly in the eyes

"If I carry you on my shoulders, will you promise not to wee on me?" He looked deadly serious, and I nodded gravely in reply, but then he smiled, tousled my hair, and laughed very loudly.

"I'm only joking Michael." He laughed again, and this time I joined in, because I understood grown up jokes now.

He lifted me on to his shoulders, hooking a strong restraining arm behind my back. He made a clicking noise with his tongue on the roof of his mouth.

"Come on then cowboy, ride me." He skipped for a couple of paces, and then stopped.

I tried to make the clicking noise, but I couldn't manage it. He put me down again, and gave me a quick riding lesson. He taught me how to use the collar of his dark blue overcoat as a pair of reins, and taught me some 'basic commands.' We had to make several stops along the way, for him to have a cigarette. But I walked, trotted, cantered and galloped him all the way into Long Ashton.

It was quite dark when we finally arrived at our destination. I could just pick out a tiny knot of people in the middle of the road. They were standing at the bottom of what turned out to be Providence Lane. They were clapping, cheering and waving. I felt like some homecoming hero.

Jacob put me down quickly but gently.

"I'm out of here." He kissed the tips of the fingertips of his right hand, and placed them tenderly on my mother's cheek. "Stay lucky and stay lovely."

He melted away into the night. I would never see him again, but for just a few brief hours I had experienced what life with a father would be like. I'd enjoyed it.

My mother had promised us a new and a better life, and this was precisely what she delivered. She and Mary were staying with Aunty Elsie and Uncle Joe. They had a neat, but small house at the very bottom of the lane. I was staying with Mrs. Sherbourne and her daughter Margaret, who lived directly opposite. They had a very large house with big rooms and a huge garden. Mrs. Sherbourne was a stout lady with a very red face and grey hair. Her daughter was aged about fourteen, and she was a big girl with a very red face and brown hair. I liked them, and they were both very kind to me. Mrs. Sherbourne described me as a 'rough diamond', but promised 'to polish me up until I was the 'finished article'. She then taught me to say grace before meals, and to always say 'please' and 'thank you'; not to snatch for the toast, but to wait until it was offered to me; to eat with a knife and fork instead of my fingers, and she told me that 'Fucking Jerry' and 'The big bastard with my name written on it', were not acceptable topics for the dinner table. After just a few weeks she gave me a hug and a big kiss, before declaring me to be a perfect gentleman. I couldn't have been happier.

Long Ashton was a lovely place, with never ending stretches of open green fields, beautiful woods, babbling brooks, songbirds, cows, rabbits and seemingly continuous sunshine. There were also wasps, stinging nettles and cow pats, but these were only minor irritants. I spent many long, happy hours with Mum. She showed me the house where she had been born and raised with her family. She took me to the school where she had learnt to read, write and recite Longfellow's Hiawatha from beginning to end. She took me to the fields where she had played with her sisters, and she showed me the big house on the hill where she had been a servant. She spoke with great affection about Lady Smyth, but she was sad again as she told me once more about the long, slow deaths of her mother and her bothers from Tuberculosis. She sat on the grass and cried, and I cried with her as I tried to comfort her.

Nothing good lasts forever, and one day, as the nights grew colder and the trees began to change colour, I woke up and I was feeling ill again. This time I was very ill. I was drifting in and out of consciousness. The same doctor called, wearing the same jacket, with the same pocketful of pens. He really was important; this time he arrived in his own ambulance. I can remember the sea of anxious faces around the bed as the doctor examined me. Mrs. Sherbourne comforted Mum as they carried me to the ambulance. We rumbled into Bristol, bound for Tower Hill Clinic, which I recognised because I had been there for x Rays when I had been ill before. Tower Hill stood like a Palace in the midst of the desert of flattened bombed building sites in Castle Street and Counterslip. I had my x Rays, and then we rumbled back to Long Ashton.

The doctor leapt out of the ambulance as soon as we arrived. Mum was already standing there, waiting. The door was half open and I watched as the doctor put his hands on her shoulders, looked her in the eyes and spoke to her. Mum was wearing a brave face, with a firm mouth, but she had worried eyes. I heard the doctor say the words 'shadows on the lungs.' As the doctor spoke, Mum's face, and her firm mouth crumpled like a rubber mask against a flame and she screamed, and then started to cry. She cried silently, sobbing with her head buried in the doctor's chest, and then he led her slowly back into the house.

The ambulance driver appeared at the open door. He was a tall, thin man, with a yellow face and matching teeth. He removed the cigarette end from the corner of his mouth, and picked a stray piece of tobacco from his tongue. He then coughed and spat.

"Who's a lucky boy?" he wheezed. "I'm taking you to the seaside."

I fell asleep.

It had come as no surprise when Mum announced that we might be moving back to Bristol. I had already seen all the warning signs. She was restless, and had been disappearing into town on a regular basis.

"I'm looking for work," was her explanation "and sorting out a school for Michael."

I knew that the beautiful butterfly was preparing to flutter her wings, and we were about to fly off again. Although Mum had spent her childhood in Long Ashton, she had grown accustomed to big city living. She was missing the daily hustle and bustle. She wanted, and needed, the excitement of the shops, the rattle of the traffic and the clamour of the crowds. More importantly there were no pawn shops in Long Ashton to help out with the weekly budget, and there were not enough men telling her that she looked like Hedy Lamarr.

She broke the news to me as we were making our way into Bristol on the bus. We were going for a picnic on Brandon Hill.

"It's a special treat for a special little boy." I didn't know what I had done to merit this, but I certainly wasn't going to argue. I liked being special, I liked treats, and I liked Brandon Hill.

"Summer is almost over, but Brandon Hill will be nice at this time of year. It will do both of us a bit of good."

She told me the bombing had all but finished; that Mr. Hitler had now sent his planes to Russia; that Father Doyle had kindly sorted me out a place at St Mary on the Quay Infant school, and that she had found us a lovely house in Kingsdown. We made our way up to the base of the Cabot Tower. I knew that Mum would be telling me some stories; there was something about Brandon Hill that always set her off. I didn't mind, because Mum was a good story teller, and it wasn't long before she started.

"This is the very spot where I met your father for the first time". She smiled and chuckled. "He was very shy."

I listened closely as she told me about my father, and his first marriage. She told me, once again, about her childhood in Long Ashton, and how she had lost her mother and her two favourite brothers to TB. I heard the story about her work at Ashton Court, about the gardener, and how her baby Ivan had been 'put up for adoption'.

"You have two brothers out there somewhere Michael. Maybe one day you can all meet up and be like real brothers."

I was interested in the stories, but I was more interested now in the picnic. The food was all neatly wrapped up in newspaper to keep the germs and the dirt out. We made our way down the crazy paved pathway; past the fish pond with the giant goldfish darting around, and then we found a bench with a nice view across Bristol. We sat and ate in contented silence. It was only bread and jam, but it was strawberry jam, and strawberry jam was my favourite.

We wandered around until Mum found a gentle slope where she tried to teach me to roly-poly. I wasn't very good at it, and by the time I eventually managed to make my way from the top to the bottom I had a fit of the giggles. Mum, took advantage, pinned me down, and blew raspberries on my neck until I was helpless with hysterical laughter and begging for mercy.

It was a nice day, one of those special days that will always stay in your memory.

But that had been several days ago, and now I was slowly waking up in a strange bed, in an unfamiliar darkened room. I could see candles flickering, and I could just pick out some vague shapes. I could hear the sound of women's voices. They were whispering and giggling in that special way that a woman does. I thought for one moment I was back in the tunnel, but then I remembered the doctor, the ambulance and Tower Hill Clinic. I felt a haunted chill run down my spine, and I started to cry. I called out for Mum, and one of the vague shapes holding one of the candles hurried in my direction. I recognised the uniform. It was a nurse, and she was young, blonde and lovely. She looked and sounded like an angel.

"Hush now Michael, you'll wake everyone." She smiled and held a finger up to her lips. "You've not been well, but we're going to make you better. I am Nurse Pamela and you are in Weston super Mare Sanatorium." She gently lifted my head, whilst at the same time expertly plumping up my pillow with her free hand.

"Here drink this." She raised a glass to my lips. It was orange juice; I loved orange juice. "Now get some sleep, I will wake you up when it's time for breakfast."

When I woke up it was light, and I could clearly see my surroundings. Nurse Pamela was by my side, smiling and watching me closely. I was in a long, narrow room with a line of beds on either wall. I was quite taken aback by the whiteness of the sheets and the pillows. On each of the pillows lay an equally white face. Some of the boys were jumping out of bed and making a dash for the wash basins which were along the walls at each end of the room. I made a move to get up, but Nurse Pamela placed a restraining arm across my chest.

"You are on full rest, young man." She pointed to the boys at the basins who were now splashing water on their faces. "Your turn will come soon enough."

I wasn't even allowed to sit up for breakfast. Nurse Pamela fed me, and I didn't mind a bit, because I was given the finest breakfast of my life. I will never forget that first meal. I had a large bowl of porridge with milk and sugar. This was followed by two rashers of bacon and a whole piece of fried bread, two rounds of toast with real butter, and two pieces of bread and butter with jam. It wasn't strawberry jam, but I wasn't complaining.

The food was so good. I can remember there were always lots of cold meats with plenty of boiled potatoes, cabbage and lots of butter. I had only ever known war time rationing, and could only dream of food like this. In fact, by the end of the first week, I had quite fallen in love with Nurse Pamela, and with Weston super Mare Sanatorium.

By the end of the second week I was on 'two pillows', but I was still not allowed to sit up. Everyone was 'on' something. Full rest, half rest, sitting up, one pillow, two pillows, walk to dining rooms. There was a list as long as your arm. I slowly got the hang of things. I don't know how long I was in that place. The days turned into weeks, and the weeks into months. I stopped looking up expectantly when the doors swung open. I no longer waited for my mother's friendly, familiar face to appear. At first I cried myself to sleep at night, and then I decided Mum had abandoned me in the same way she had abandoned Ivan. I willed myself to forget, and to hate her. I waited patiently for the day I would be adopted

I was on 'full exercise' now. This entailed two long walks every day. We were wrapped up against the elements, and marched the entire length of Weston super Mare beach. We walked two abreast, in silence, and with a nurse at each end of the line. The nurses shepherded us away from any casual bystanders. Old faces would disappear overnight, and new ones would spring up from nowhere. I was an old hand now; I was like an old lag in prison. I knew all the routines, and all the little tricks. I knew which faces would fall for a sweet smile, and which hearts were cold and unyielding.

It came as a bolt from the blue when Nurse Pamela told me I was better, and my mother was coming to collect me. I suddenly realised I didn't want to leave. The nurses had become my mother now, and the hospital had become my home. There were tears, tantrums and stamping of feet, but eventually I was dressed and led outside. I genuinely didn't recognise the beautiful woman who was waiting across the road. She had deep auburn hair and green eyes. She was carrying a shopping bag, and a young girl was standing by her side. The young girl had two plaits which were secured by pink ribbon. She was nervously playing with the hem of her pink and white, candy striped dress, as she bit her lower lip, swayed her shoulders from side to side, and studied me from lowered eyes.

I was clinging like a limpet to Nurse Pamela's thigh. The stranger with the auburn hair smiled, reached out and beckoned me to come to her. I knew that smile, but I clung even more tightly to the nurse's leg, and backed away.

"My God!" The woman held her hand to her mouth. I remembered Mum used to say that and hold her hand to her mouth just like that. I was weakening now.

"I thought you'd like a bag of fish and chips, I was going to buy you one." My resolve weakened further.

Then the stranger started to cry as she rummaged around in her shopping bag. She produced an old tennis ball, and a small crumpled photo of a young man wearing football kit. I didn't need to look; I knew there was a message scribbled on the back, and I knew exactly what it read. I fell into Mum's arms.

Whenever we had moved on to better things, Mum had always said 'Don't look back. The future is right in front of us, so that's where we look.' I didn't look back as we marched off down the promenade, and I didn't lag behind either.

"Slow down, there's no hurry," said Mum, but there was; I wanted to claim my prize. I wanted my bag of fish and chips.

There were a number of unanswered questions arising from my time in the hospital. It was many years later before I asked Mum about it. I was in my thirties, and she was in her fifties. She had kept the secret well. In 1941, her son had been taken to hospital, having been diagnosed with TB. Her biggest nightmare had become a reality. There was no cure for TB back then, and a stigma surrounded sufferers, even recovered patients were treated like Lepers.

I had been in hospital for eight months. I asked her why she hadn't visited me.

"You were in isolation. I visited you every week, but I couldn't come in; I wasn't allowed. Instead, I stood in the shadows, just out of view, and I watched you walking. I walked with you back and forth and I was holding your hand for every step of the way."

It only takes a second for your world to turn upside down, but it takes a lot longer to rebuild it. The Sanatorium at Weston super Mare had become my home; it was my comfort zone. Now I was struggling in a strange new world, with two people I could barely remember. The fish and chips had been great, but as we boarded the bus to return to Bristol I was feeling lost and insecure. I should have been excited and happy, but I was sad and somewhat fearful.

The journey home felt never ending. Mary curled up on Mum's lap and fell asleep, the bus rumbled on and on and on, and Mum was chatting non-stop. I think she sensed that some of my memories had faded, and she started telling me stories. They were only little stories, but they slowly and surely filled in most of the gaps that had developed in my memory.

She soon had my full attention, and I noticed a few of the other passengers were leaning forward and listening intently. She spoke about our time at Badminton Road. We all chuckled as she described how I had marched with the Salvation Army Band on Sunday mornings. We all smiled as she talked about those sun filled days in St James' Churchyard, where I used to feed the birds with the bread crumbs. She even revived a bad memory. She reminded me of the day when I had stolen an apple from the Greengrocer's display in Gloucester Road. We had reached the bottom of Stokes Croft before I produced it from my pocket, and Mum had then marched me all the way back to return it and apologise.

"Having a thief in the family would break my heart."

She didn't mention Mr. Burke or Mrs. Grant, but then again, she didn't need to, because I had very clear memories of them both, along with my memories of the Military Police..

She spoke fondly about our days at Kingsdown Parade. She recalled how Peggy and I ran down the road juggling the freshly baked loaves of bread. They were blisteringly hot and we struggled to hold on to them.

She fell silent for a while, and then revealed that Mr. Lloyd and his family had been buried alive on the night of the Good Friday raid. She rapidly added that they had been rescued, and were all alive and well. She placed her free hand around my shoulders and pulled me closer as she spoke about the blitz, and those long, frightening hours in the tunnel. For one terrible moment I feared that the other passengers on the bus were about to hear about the night when I had wet both the bunk and Mr. Brookes, but Mum didn't let me down.

She touched briefly on Long Ashton, raising her voice to announce that I had been in hospital with a bout of pneumonia. The lady in an adjoining seat promptly gave me a sweet. Mum didn't mention Jacob, but again, she didn't need to. I had clear memories of him teaching me to ride on his back, and of him kissing his fingertips before placing them tenderly on Mum's cheek.

By the time we arrived in Bristol, all my memories were safely stored back inside my head, and most of the people on the bus knew my life story.

As a very small child I had often struggled to sleep, and Mum would sing me a lullaby. One of my favourites was a song called the longest mile is the last mile home. I had never quite understood the meaning of the words in the past, but now, as we trudged wearily up Lower Maudlin Street and past the Bristol Royal Infirmary, those words made sense. It felt as if we had been walking forever.

"We're almost there. You are going to love it Michael." We were staring up Marlborough Hill.

I felt as if we were looking up the side of a mountain.

"Come on Michael, it's onwards and upwards." We started walking again.

What neither of us knew as we headed for our final destination was that Mum was taking me to a place where I would spend the happiest days of my life.

Halsbury Road was a neat little, cobblestoned cul-de-sac situate about three parts of the way up the hill, on the left hand side. There were twelve houses; six on either side of the road. The houses were tall, slender, red bricked buildings which rose elegantly into the Kingsdown skies. They were four floors high, with two rooms on each level. There were even two front doors. There was one on the ground floor, and another on the first floor. This latter door was reached by way of climbing an imposing, external grey slated staircase. The metal railings had been removed for the 'war effort', and Mum was quick to ban me from using the stairs.

Up until now, we'd spent the whole of our life living in a couple of tiny rooms and an even smaller kitchen. I never did discover how my mother managed to gain control of a complete house, and I was too tired to ask any questions that night. Mum made up a fire, and I curled up in the armchair, and fell asleep.

You always hurt the one you love,
The one you shouldn't hurt at all,
You always break the kindest heart
With a hasty word you can't recall.

Mum was on her hands and knees polishing the red flagstone floor in the hallway of our new house. She was singing at the top of her voice as she polished. She had her back to me, and was completely unaware of my presence. I liked it when Mum was singing. I sat on the bottom stair as I watched and listened.

So if I broke your heart last night
It's because I love you most of all.

She finished polishing with a flourish of the duster, and finished singing with a big note. She stood up, yawned and stretched.

"Please, please Lord give me strength." She turned and jumped, startled as she saw me sitting there. "Look at you, half naked and just out of hospital with pneumonia." She took my hand and led me into the living room.

"Just look at me." She was studying herself closely in the mirror. "Now we have a house, I have to become a housewife."

She knelt in front of me, looking me in the eyes. "And, until your father gets home, you will have to be the man of the house."

I liked the sound of that, because Mum had already told me that the 'man of the house' always had the biggest portions of food.

My clothes were all hanging from the back of a chair in front of the roaring fire. She dressed me quickly; it was just like old times. I stood there, looking around and taking in my new surroundings. The same old clock was on the mantle shelf, with Dad's photo tucked away behind it.

Mum was scrubbing away behind my ears with the piece of roughened towel, some spit and the tiniest piece of soap. She was complaining about the soap being rationed. We were off to St Mary on the Quay Infant School. I needed to be registered, and I needed to look my best. Father Doyle would be there waiting for us, and we were running late.

We were soon running even later. We had barely passed the

Bristol Royal Infirmary when the jeep pulled up alongside us. Bristol had changed a lot whilst I had been away. Amongst other things the drab, grey streets had changed. Overnight, or so it seemed, those streets had changed into a more glamorous version of Hollywood in Technicolor. There were American soldiers everywhere. Brash, confident, handsome young men, all wearing smart uniforms, and looking and sounding like film stars. The young soldier who vaulted out of the jeep was one of them. He was tall and slim, with a gleaming white smile. He clicked his heels, and saluted us. I saluted back, and he burst out laughing as he removed his cap and stood in front of us.

"Good morning ma'am. We would like to give your young brother a packet of gum. I hope you don't mind." He tossed me a packet of chewing gum, and Mum nervously started to explain that I wasn't her brother. She had only just started speaking when they both started laughing, and then they moved a little way up the road. They stood smoking, laughing and talking for several minutes. I was struggling with the packaging on the chewing gum, and one of the other American soldiers jumped from the jeep and helped me out.

"His name was Buddy...what a lovely name." We were hurrying up Perry Road now. Mum was wearing that look on her face; the Hedy Lamarr look. It was the look that usually spelled trouble.

"He thought I was your sister... Do I really look that young?"

I didn't reply. I just knew there was indeed trouble looming ahead.

We were late, and Father Doyle was looking less than pleased when we walked in. He was waiting with three Nuns, Sisters Philomena, Josephine and Geraldine. They ran the Infant School and they were all very nice, but I liked Sister Josephine the best. She put me on her lap whilst Mum spoke with the others. She had a book, and we did some reading. Sister Josephine pursed her lips and nodded at Mum.

"He's good, you've done very well."

Mum took me in to the pawn shop on the way home, and I met Mr. Keeler for the first time. She introduced me to him and he called me 'young man.' He wasn't at all what I had been expecting. He was a very small man. He wore spectacles, had very white hair, and spoke with a very quiet voice. To my surprise he didn't look or sound very important and he only had a single pen in his breast pocket. He had plenty of money though. He studied Mum's engagement ring closely, through a tiny eye piece, and then smiled, nodded and gave her a silver coin and a ticket.

Mum was happy. "That's supper sorted."

It was just like old times. I lay in front of the fire listening to ITMA, and I joined in the applause from the studio audience as the great man was introduced.

"Calling all hand to muster; blunt razors to plaster; the Wren shook her head when I asked her." Tommy Handley rattled out his lines without hesitation. He was very good.

The audience roared with laughter, and I joined in, but my laughter was halfhearted. I was just a little bit annoyed, because I didn't understand the joke, and I had convinced myself that I had mastered the art of adult humour.

It was a good night though. We had cheese and chips for supper and life was good.

4 WE WILL HAVE ROSES IN THE SUMMER

I was five now and feeling quite grown up. I was fully ready for my new role as the 'man of the house'. Mum told me that I had missed a birthday whilst I had been in hospital, and she gave me a belated present. It was something I had long been nagging her for; a pen knife. The handle was in mother of pearl, and there were two blades. I was pleased with my knife, and with my birthday bread pudding that Mum had made for me. I felt somewhat guilty about drawing Mum's attention to the porridge, egg, bacon, sausage, fried bread and toast breakfasts that Nurse Pamela used to give me in the Sanatorium. Mum quietly and patiently tried to explain 'rationing' to me, and how it worked. I still didn't fully understand it, but she told me we were only allowed one egg per person per week, and two rashers of bacon per person per fortnight.

"We just have to take the rough with the smooth, and be grateful for small mercies." Mum had a saying for everything, and it always made sense.

There was a further advantage to being the 'man of the house'. I was given first choice of whichever room I wanted for my bedroom. I felt like an explorer as I poked and prodded my way around the house. I inspected every nook, cranny and corner of every single room. When I finally announced my decision Mum was horrified. I had selected the one room in the house that was not in good order. To be honest, it was in a very poor condition. The pink flowered wall paper and the plaster were both peeling away from the walls, and three large buckets were strategically placed in one corner of the room to collect the rainwater which was dripping constantly from the leaking roof. Mum did her best to persuade me to change my mind, but all to no avail. It was the view from the window of that fourth floor room that had made my mind up; it was quite breath-taking. Living up there I felt like a young millionaire in a pent house, and when I looked out of that window I felt like a young prince surveying my future kingdom. On a fine clear day I could see the whole of East Bristol

Mum said the other side of the road was the 'posh side'. This was because the houses had a coat of paint on the doors, and flowers and shrubs in the tiny, but neat front gardens. I never forgot Mum's words and for the remainder of my days in the street, I always looked up to Mr. and Mrs. Knight, Mr. and Mrs. Miller and Mrs. Annie Cole. I regarded them as my superiors. If I had worn a cap, I would have doffed it to them.

"When your father comes home we will have paint on the doors and the windows, and we will have flowers in the garden." Mum was on her hands and knees as she spoke. She was cutting the grass in our front garden with a pair of nail scissors. "We will have roses in the summer and bluebells in the spring."

I didn't have the pen knife for long. It was confiscated within a few weeks. Firstly, I cut my mouth trying to open the blade with my teeth, and the Doctor at the Bristol Royal Infirmary had a stern face and a serious voice as he told Mum I was too young to have such a toy. Mum issued me with a final warning when we got home. Just a few days later she arrived back from the shops to find a terrified Mary standing with her arms outstretched, and her back to the door, whilst I hurled the knife at her. I was attempting to emulate the knife throwing act we had recently seen at the cinema. The knife disappeared into Mum's handbag and I never saw it again.

"Got any gum chum?" I was standing, with Mary, in the entrance to the Hippodrome. We were sheltering from a heavy shower. School had finished early and there was some time to kill before Mum arrived to pick us up. We had made our way down to the Tramway Centre. I had already made a promise to myself that I would never ask any American soldiers for chewing gum, but I was bored, and hungry. I could feel myself weakening, and right on cue the two soldiers came wandering by. Only a few nights earlier I had heard a man on the radio describing American soldiers as being 'overpaid, oversexed and over here.' He didn't seem to like them very much, and whilst I didn't wholly understand his views, I had found myself disliking them as well. The two soldiers to whom I had addressed my request stopped and stared at me.

"Got any gum chum?" I was demanding now, growing in confidence.

The shorter and plumper one of the two took a packet of chewing gum from his pocket, and dangled it invitingly under my nose. "That all depends." He leant forward, waving the gum temptingly. He pointed at Mary. "Have you got an older sister?"

"Or even an attractive mother?" The other soldier joined in.

'Overpaid, oversexed and over here.' I felt quite proud of myself as I turned and walked slowly away. I would never ask another soldier for chewing gum again.

Mum had three jobs. She had a cleaning job at a lady's house in Archfield Road, Cotham, and two others, both in Park Row. The first involved cleaning in the Jewish Synagogue; the other was directly across the road from there, where she washed dishes in a restaurant.

"It's either that or we will have to take in lodgers," She said the words sadly, and I quickly nodded approvingly. I didn't want any strangers coming into my castle.

It all worked out quite nicely. Mum would start the day by taking us to school, and then cleaning the Synagogue. The Synagogue was massive and I was very proud that my mother was cleaning the entire building. She would then head off up Horfield Road for the second cleaning job in Cotham. The restaurant where Mum washed the dishes was almost next to the school, so it was all very easy for her.

Our next door neighbour was Mrs. Norris. She was a tall, thin lady with very long, very black hair and not many teeth. She always wore a loose fitting, blue flowered dress and always had a cigarette dangling from the corner of her mouth. Whenever she spoke, she coughed. Mrs. Norris didn't have any jobs, but she did have lodgers. The current lodgers were Nancy and Ken. They were Welsh so I presumed they were from Newport. I liked Aunty Nancy, but Mum wasn't 'too sure' about her. Mum also said that Uncle Ken was a 'spiv'. I suspected that Mum didn't like Aunty Nancy because she was very pretty, and she had long shiny brown hair, large breasts and a big smile. I liked her because she gave me sweets and spoke to me. Uncle Ken had ginger hair, a small ginger moustache and he rode a motor bike. He made tiny toy windmills, which were made of small, coloured pieces of plastic attached to thin pieces of wood. Mum said he drove his motor bike to the seaside every day and sold the 'rubbish' to children.

I was proud and happy to be at St Mary on the Quay school. My mother told me that my father had attended that very school as a young boy, and she had promised him that I would follow in his footsteps. I was in the Infants, and Mary was at the Nursery. Sister Josephine was very kind and taught me reading, writing and arithmetic. I liked the reading and writing, but I didn't enjoy the arithmetic, and I didn't enjoy playtimes either. In addition to being the Nursery and the Infants school, St Mary's was also the 'big girls' school. The playground was always a sea of screaming, shouting, chanting girls. They were all skipping, hopping and arguing as they bounced and threw balls against the walls. None of them ever played football, and I would drift off to the bottom of the yard, lean over the wall, and watch the big boys playing football in the Trenchard Street playground below.

A boy called 'Moggy' was my hero. He was a short boy with dark hair. He may have been short in stature but in terms of footballing ability he was huge. He wore cut down wellington boots, which must have been an enormous disadvantage, but he had complete control of that tiny tennis ball. I studied him closely and noted how he always drifted away from the heaving mass of boys chasing the ball around the yard. When the ball finally squirted loose from the scrimmage, Moggy was always there with time and space to wrap his instep around the ball and deliver it accurately to his chosen destination. I dreamt of going to the 'big boys' school and being on the same side as Moggy.

As the afternoons wore on, I would grow tired, and Sister Josephine would cradle me in her arms, and sing to me. She always sang the same lullaby. She sang softly and gently, as she rocked me until I fell asleep.

My Mother sang a song to me
In tones so sweet and low;
Just a simple little ditty,

In her good old Irish way,
And I'd give the world to hear her sing
That song of hers today.

Toora-loora-looral, Toora-loo-ra-li,
Toora-loora-looral, Hush now don't you cry!
Toora-loora-looral, Toora-loora-li,
Toora-loora-looral, that's an Irish lullaby

When I woke up it was usually time to go home. Mary and I would sit on the steps outside of the school, as we waited for Mum to finish her final job of the day. Mum was always on time, but one day she was late. We waited and waited until eventually, I told Mary to stay where she was whilst I went off to investigate. I went outside and looked up the road. I saw her straight away. She was standing outside of the Red Lodge. She was laughing and joking with an American soldier. He looked familiar; I recognised him as the soldier who had vaulted from the jeep to speak to us all those weeks earlier. It was the same one who had scribbled a note on the packet of cigarettes. I struggled to remember his name.

'His name was Buddy…what a lovely name'.

He was lighting a cigarette for her. His hand was cupped across the cigarette protecting the flame of his lighter from the breeze. His long fingers were touching her cheek. It was like going back in time to that day in St James Churchyard. It was like watching her with Mr. Burke again. The alarm bells started to ring. I turned, walked back to Mary, and put my arm around her.

"She's on her way." Mary just continued playing with her little knitted doll. She ignored me and didn't reply. I think she still hadn't quite forgiven me for the knife throwing episode.

I had already learnt that nothing good lasts forever, and that the world was a constantly changing place, and now I was learning that life was a fascinating mixture of good times and bad times; a delicately balanced cocktail of laughter and tears.

I asked Mum about the meeting with Buddy. She laughed it off and described it as 'pure chance'. She said that he was often in that area, and they frequently bumped in to one another.

We had settled in very nicely at Halsbury Road. Mum had been quick to point out to us that everything we needed was right there on our doorstep. Mr. Keeler's pawn shop was at the bottom of the hill, the Bristol Co-operative Grocery stores were at the top of the hill, and right next door to that building was Smith's Fish and Chip shop. Parker's Bakery was only a short walk along Kingsdown Parade, and there were even two sweet shops within easy walking distance. Mrs. Moore's shop was the closest of the two at the top of Alfred Hill, but I had never forgotten the extra sherbet lemon that Mrs. Tuck had slipped into the bag on that day when Mum had received the telegram from the Admiralty. Increasingly more in hope than expectation, I usually ended up in Mrs. Tuck's shop, but my loyalty was never rewarded again.

It was summer time now, and we were on holiday from school. The sun seemed to shine down on us all day and every day. I had risen early that morning. It was so early that I witnessed my first ever sunrise. I stood at the window and watched wide eyed with amazement as that ball of fire lit up the skies as it came into view over the hills of Purdown. I then took my tennis ball out on to the hill for more football practice. I had long since discovered that the more I practiced, the better I got. My practice drill was simplicity itself. I hurled the ball up the hill and watched with a mixture of excitement, fear and apprehension as it came bouncing back down at me, gathering pace, as it spat and reared off the cobblestones. If I missed it, I was faced with a chase down that steep hill. Sometimes, the chase would take me all the way down to the bottom, and would often then take me across Marlborough Street and all the way down Whitson Street to where the buses now exit from the Coach Station. There were many back to back misses, but I had persevered. Those chases and long trudges back up the hill were great incentives to improve, and I had now reached a point where I seldom missed. I had improved to the point where I could now occasionally wrap my instep around the ball and volley it back from whence it came. Moggy, without even knowing it, had taught me well. I was ready now to join his team.

Mum was taking Mary to work with her, and I elected to stay at home. I'd taken a few sheets and blankets down to Mr. Keeler's shop on the previous day, and we therefore had some money, but we were still without food, and Mum sat studying our ration books. She sat in silence, rubbing her chin and looking worried. She grimaced, groaned and then broke the news to me. We had somehow managed to use up our weekly quota. We weren't entitled to any further rations until the following week. Mum scribbled out a shopping list on a piece of scrap paper, wrapped it around Mr. Keeler's two shilling piece, and dispatched me off to the Co-op.

"You must see Mr. Morris; nobody else will do". She handed me one of the ration books, and repeated the instructions, slowly and clearly.

I liked going to the Co-op. There was sawdust on the highly polished floors, and over the top of each counter was a fascinating gadget, where the counter assistant would put your money and a ticket into one half of a cup. This was then attached to the other half of the cup that was suspended on a wire line. The line ran the full length of the shop from the counter to a small office which was raised to a higher level. A lady cashier sat in the office. After attaching the cup to the wire the assistant would pull down on a handle and the cup would shoot along the wire to the cashier. She would then write in a book before returning the cup, together with any change and a ticket. There were several of these wire gadgets operated from each counter by assistants serving different customers.

I waited in the long queue with a lot of ladies who were waiting to see Mr. Morris. He was clearly a very popular man. He was short and stocky, with a fat face, an even fatter stomach and slicked back, well-oiled hair. He always wore a sparklingly clean white coat, and there were pens and pencils galore bursting out of his breast pocket. I think he might have been Welsh, but I wasn't certain about that. I stood and waited patiently until it was my turn.

"Good morning Master Kelly." Mr. Morris started whistling as he unwrapped and read Mum's note. He fell silent as he quickly studied the ration book, and then took a glance around over his shoulders. He whipped a short stubby pencil from his pocket, licked the end, and quickly waved it over the page as if he were drawing a line across the book.

"How's your mother?" He expertly pulled the piece of wire across a slab of butter, and then followed suit on a piece of cheese. He wrapped up the two small portions in greaseproof paper.

"Mum is well." I mumbled nervously. I was now in a hurry to get out of the shop. I was fully expecting the police to arrive and arrest me at any minute.

"Make sure you give her my love," The overhead container whizzed its way towards the cashier's office. "And make sure to tell her I haven't seen her around lately." The container thudded back into its place above the counter. Mr. Morris unscrewed the half, removed my change, and handed it to me. He smiled, nodded and started whistling again as he returned my ration book, and handed me the small white paper bag that contained the food.

He was rubbing his hands together again and smiling as he greeted the next lady in the queue. "Hello my love. I haven't seen you around lately."

I hung around and watched closely as she nervously handed her ration book to him. He glanced equally nervously over his shoulders, took the pencil from his pocket, and licked it before pretending to cross off the relevant section in the book. I ran home quickly. I didn't want to be around when the policeman came.

Despite everything, I quite liked Mr. Morris. His food was very good; he whistled some good tunes, and he always had a big smile on his face.

There was only the one problem with life at Halsbury Road, but it was a big problem. It was the very same old problem that had followed me around Bristol. There were no other children in the road. There was no one to play with, apart from the two older girls who lived in number 7. The elder of the two, Pamela, bore a striking resemblance to Peggy Woodruff. She was tall and slender, and like Peggy, she also had very large feet. She was also very kind to me, but I fell out of favour on the day I invited her to play 'doctors and nurses'. She ran off indoors, before returning to tell me she was no longer allowed to play with me. Her mother gave me a long and very funny look when she next saw me in the street.

I had already asked Mum's permission to go further afield in pursuit of friendships. She hesitated before giving her approval. And the approval when it came was conditional.

"Trouble doesn't travel up a hill. If you go anywhere, you go that way." She pointed up the hill in the direction of Kingsdown Parade.

And so it was that on that sunny morning in August 1942, I set off in search of friendship and adventure. . There were many bombed building sites at the top of the hill, but I was particularly interested in one of them. Directly at the top of the hill, on the other side of the road was a large brick wall which bounded the back garden of what had been a big house in Montague Place. The house itself was opposite the Headquarters of the Royal Gloucester Hussars Regiment. Both of the buildings had been destroyed in the blitz.

There was a big green door in the centre of that brick wall, which would tantalisingly open for just a few inches; not quite far enough to allow even a child of my age and size to enter. On that day the road was deserted; there was no one around, so I gently applied some pressure with my shoulder. Suddenly there was a slight movement. It was not a lot, but suddenly there was space, just sufficient space for me to be able to squeeze my way in. I found myself in a world where I was completely alone. I was in a magical, special place where there were no prying eyes, no one to shatter the peace, no one to interrupt your thoughts. It was a wonderful place, and it was mine, and mine alone. There were several large piles of bricks and debris, but there was still beauty everywhere. There were flowers of many different types and colours, shrubs and ornamental grasses; an empty fish pond and some ornate wrought iron garden furniture.

I ventured rather nervously into the house itself, but I didn't linger inside for long. The staircase was all but totally destroyed, and the floorboards were almost non-existent. The entire house felt as if it were on the verge of total collapse. I returned to the garden and sat on an old wooden bench in the shade of a bent and withered tree. The bench was set against a wall which ran for the entire length of the garden. A bush which was bursting with a red berried fruit dominated the remainder of the wall. Mum had lectured me long and often about the dangers of eating strange berries, so I only had five or six of them, even though they were delicious.

I felt at peace with the world, but it didn't last for long. Panic suddenly set in, as I recalled Mum's dramatic descriptions of the perils of eating strange berries. I remembered how she had told me about the pains, the sickness and the long drawn out agonies of the inevitable death. I picked several more berries and rushed home with them.

Mum and Mary were home from the cleaning, and were now preparing to go to the shops. I showed Mum the berries, but I didn't mention that I had eaten some. Mum immediately put one into her mouth, and then stood still, with her eyes closed, moaning gently as she slowly chewed it.

"Michael, you little beauty, they're raspberries. Where did you find them?"

I pointed up the hill, "Bombed building site." I waited for my punishment; instead mum dashed off and returned with two empty shoe boxes. "Pick as many as you can. We will have some for tea, and I will make jam with the rest."

Mum and Mary went down the hill, heading for the shops, and I marched back up the hill to complete my raspberry picking. All was well in Halsbury Road, I just needed some friends.

I picked away solidly for about an hour. By the time I'd finished, both of the shoe boxes and my stomach were very full. I rested on my bench and made some plans. Father Doyle would be calling in later, and Mum was going to ask him if I could join the choir. She was also going to ask him if I could move to the 'big boy's school' next term. Sister Josephine had told her my reading and writing were 'coming along nicely'.

I was just making my way out of the garden when I noticed it. The sun was reflecting from an object in the pile of debris I had disturbed when I had opened the green gate. I pulled away at the loose earth and removed a brick or two. I'd struck gold; I had uncovered a tin of biscuits. The label was still intact, but the lid was buckled, damaged by the weight of the debris. I tried hard, but I couldn't remove it. I wasn't unduly worried; my day was getting better and better. We now had both raspberries and biscuits for tea.

Mum and Mary weren't back from the shops, and the key wasn't in its usual place in the coal house, so I climbed up the forbidden outside stairs and waited as I let the afternoon sun beat down on my head, and I drifted off to sleep.

"What have you got there?" It was Aunty Nancy, standing over me.

"They're raspberries." I pushed the shoe boxes a little further away from her. I liked Aunty Nancy, but the boxes were emptying at an alarming rate. I had developed a taste for raspberries.

"Not those…the tin." She pointed to my biscuits.

"Biscuits," I replied, "but I can't open the lid."

"Give them here." Aunty Nancy leant across the wall and took the tin from my hands.

She opened the lid straight away. I stood up and we both stared at the contents. I experienced the bitter taste of disappointment. The blood drained from Aunty Nancy's face. There were no biscuits. The tin was full of bank notes. There were green notes, brown notes and white ones. All in neat bundles, secured with paper clips. As a child in a house where the largest unit currency was normally a half crown coin, the notes meant little to me. I would have gladly swopped them for biscuits.

"Where did you find this?" She could barely speak.

"I found it in the bombed building site." I waved my arm up the hill, in the direction of Kingsdown Parade.

Nancy was breathing heavily now. "Has your mother seen this?"

I shook my head slowly.

"Then she never must. It would break her heart to know that her son was a thief. This is stealing, and that makes you a thief Michael. You could go to prison."

I didn't like the sound of that. I had heard on the radio that prisoners were fed on bread and water. I had a big problem, but Aunty Nancy had a solution for it.

"Listen closely Michael. Ken and I will take this to Bridewell in the morning. We will say that we found it in the street. We won't mention your name, and you won't get into any trouble, but you mustn't under any circumstances mention it to your mother."

She ran up the stairs and took the tin into the house. She returned and gave me a sweet.

"Remember...not a word. If it's claimed, there could well be a reward."

I didn't say a word to Mum when she got back from the shops. We had raspberries for tea. Mum poured some milk over them, sprinkled them with sugar. Mum boiled the remainder and showed me how to make jam.

"You've done well today Michael."

I went to bed that night and dreamt about 'rewards'. I kept pictured Mum's smiling face as I handed her the two shilling piece.

I didn't see Aunty Nancy or Uncle Ken for several weeks, and slowly my dream of a reward faded away. It was about a month later when Mum dropped the bombshell. We were sharing a portion of fish and chips. There were only two chips remaining, and they were both on the end of Mum's fork. I was hoping they were going to find their way on to my plate. Mum looked as if she had something on her mind; she was miles away.

"I always knew they had money." She waved her fork in the direction of next door, and then swallowed the chips. It wasn't my day.

"That Ken and Nancy, from next door" She continued, "He came home today in a new car. They've bought a house in Cornwall. They've moved out, they're gone."

I never told Mum about that biscuit tin, I've never told anyone... until now.

5 IN THE MOOD

"Blessed are the poor in spirit: for theirs is the kingdom of heaven.

Blessed are the meek: for they shall possess the land.

Blessed are they that mourn: for they shall be comforted."

Father Doyle was in full flow as he stood before us and roared out the Eight Beatitudes. Mum, Mary and I were scattered around the room, we were all kneeling, with our hands clasped together in prayer. Mum was slightly behind the priest, and she was being naughty. She was peeping at me with one eye open, and pulling faces. I wanted to giggle, but Father Doyle was staring straight at me, and I somehow managed to keep a straight face.

"Blessed are they that hunger and thirst after justice: for they shall have their fill.

Blessed are the merciful: for they shall obtain mercy.

Blessed are the clean of heart: for they shall see God." Mum pretended to look at her watch. I knew she wasn't wearing it, because I had taken it to Mr. Keeler's that very day.

"Blessed are the peacemakers: for they shall be called children of God.

Blessed are they that suffer persecution for justice' sake: for theirs is the kingdom of heaven.

Blessed are ye when they shall revile you, and persecute you, and speak all that is evil against you, untruly, for my sake: Be glad and rejoice, for your reward is very great in heaven."

Father Doyle was done now; he stopped shouting at us, and made the sign of the cross. We, all three, copied him. I was impressed that Father Doyle knew all those beatitudes off by heart. He didn't have to read any of them.

Mum stood up, thanked him, and offered him a cup of tea. He said 'Yes please', and asked for 'no sugar'. He was a very strange man; the only man I had ever known who didn't take sugar. He didn't smoke either, and Mum told me that Catholic priests never got married. I wondered who cooked their meals, washed their clothes and washed and dried their dishes. I wondered who cleaned and polished their floors, and who sang them their lullabies? There had been a time in my short life when I had harboured ambitions to become a Catholic priest, but I was slowly changing my mind.

Father Doyle had, however brought good news with him. I had been accepted into the choir, and from now on I would be attending the junior school in Trenchard Street. I was very pleased and excited about that, because I would now be playing football with my hero, Moggy.

I had been preparing myself for joining the choir. I had been regularly attending Mass on Sunday mornings, and I had learnt a lot of Latin. I also now knew exactly when to sit, stand or kneel, and when to shout 'Amen'. I made sure that I always sat behind Rosie Tedesco at the back of the church. She was Italian, and she had an amazing voice. Her voice was even better than Mum's, and she sang very, very loudly. This enabled me to sing at the top of my voice, secure in the knowledge that no one would hear me if I made a mistake.

Father Doyle explained to us that I would be paid one shilling for my services. This would be paid at the end of each year, and would be dependent on my attending both Mass and choir practice on a regular basis.

After Father Doyle had left, Mum taught Mary some reading and writing whilst I listened to the radio. At nine o'clock we all fell silent as we sat together and listened to Alvar Lidell reading the Nine O'clock News.

I felt a moment of panic as Alvar told us about a disastrous convoy mission to Malta. The convoy had been decimated by U Boats and HMS Eagle, one of our biggest boats had been sunk. Only a handful of merchant ships had made it through.

"He will be alright; we would have heard something by now."

Mum must have read my thoughts.

Alvar also told us that General Bernard Montgomery had been appointed commander of British Eighth Army in North Africa; he added that Mr. Churchill was anxious to see more offensive action on the part of the British. The Luftwaffe was bombing Stalingrad. I felt sorry for the Russians and hoped they had a good tunnel to hide in. I wondered whether they had someone like Jacob on the door.

"I think the tide is about to turn. We will be OK now that we have the Americans on board." Mum spoke up; I stared at her, and she blushed. Mary had already told me that she and Mum had been speaking to an American soldier when they had last gone shopping.

Mary went off to bed, and Mum taught me some naughty poems. I particularly remember how we both laughed loudly as she taught me there was a young lady from Ealing, and there was a young lady from Hitchen.

I went to bed shortly after, and I had nice dreams. I dreamt I was in church and I was singing Ave Maria with Rosie Tedesco. The dream got even better when Father Doyle gave me a one shilling piece.

It was all change in Halsbury Road. Mrs. Barnes moved in to number 1, which had been empty. She was a blonde lady. She had a young baby, but no husband.

"She keeps herself to herself." Mum had tried and failed to make friends with her.

Next door in number 12, Nancy and Ken were replaced by Skippy and Eileen. Skippy wasn't the man's real name, but a nickname that Mum had given him. Skippy had a very bad limp, hence the nickname, and Mum said he was a 'dirty old man.' I didn't think he was that old, but Eileen was very young. Skippy had black hair, he was short and thin, and he had a face like a weasel. I liked him; he always smiled at me, and always either spoke or nodded, as he limped past me. Eileen rarely showed her face outside of the door.

"At best, she's barely out of school." I overheard Mum whispering over the fence to Mrs. Norris.

Their bedroom was next to mine, and they certainly made a lot of noise in bed, as did Mr. Ball in number 10. Mr. Ball seemed to spend all day smoking, and all night coughing. What with the rain water constantly dripping into the buckets, Mr. Ball coughing, and Skippy and Eileen screaming, grunting and moaning, my sleep was suffering.

I told Mum, and she promised to speak to Mrs. Norris about it. Before she could, the policemen came and took Skippy away. Later that morning a man and lady called to pick up Eileen.

"Her parents I presume," said Mum.

I asked Mum about the policemen, because I hadn't realised you could get into trouble for making a noise in bed. She just laughed, but didn't explain anything.

Skippy and Eileen were replaced by Mr. and Mrs. Muldowney. They were Irish; it seemed to me that every other person in Bristol were either Irish, Welsh or Italian.

"Knock ee in Kell." Moggy delivered an inch perfect cross and I scored another goal. I loved it at big school, and I loved it when Moggy called me Kell. He came running across to me with a big grin on his face, winked and shook my hand. "I'll create em; you score em."

Mr. Stirrup rang the bell, we all drifted in slowly. "Get a move on boys," shouted Mr. Stirrup. It was time to start learning again.

My teacher was Miss Lynch, and I loved, feared and respected her in equal proportions. She was also Irish, and she was a short, sturdily built lady with frizzy black hair. She wore horn rimmed spectacles, and she always dressed in very thick woolen jumpers and long tweed skirts which ensured that no part of her body was ever on view. She was able to freeze my soul with a single scathing glance, or melt my heart with her smile. She had a voice like velvet, and she taught me well. It wasn't long before I was copying her flowing copperplate handwriting, and we sat and read Charles Dickens's novels together. We were currently reading David Copperfield.

Choir practice was on Wednesday nights, and Mr. Fiando always played the organ, he was Italian, and he played well. I will never forget the magic of those choir practices, with the sound of the music booming from the organ, and all those voices echoing around the empty church. After the practice, I would wander across the Tramway Centre to College Green. The Centre would be coming to life now; the girls and the American soldiers were both coming out to play.

College Green was the home of live music and dancing. I would find a quiet corner, and lie with my head cradled in my hands, waiting for the action. The bandstand was at the far end, roughly where City

Hall now is. The musicians were all American soldiers and they would straggle in, and set up their music stands. After removing the instruments from their cases, they would just stand there playing random notes, whilst laughing and joking amongst themselves.

The crowd would be built up very quickly. They mainly consisted of women and young girls, with the American soldiers mingling amongst them. The band conductor would always be the last to arrive, looking brisk and business-like. When he arrived, the laughing and joking stopped; the band would fall silent.

The conductor would always turn the pages of his music, abruptly issue his instructions and tap his baton on the metal music stand.

"One, two – One, two, three, four" The music started; it was always 'In the Mood', the amazing Glenn Miller tune, which I had heard on the radio. The sound of the trumpets and the saxophones echoed around the Green. I lay, watching in awe, as within seconds, the green grass would be swarming with dancing girls. They were jitter bugging, legs and underwear all on show. The American soldiers were circling, like hunters surrounding their prey. Then they moved in, and within minutes, most of the girls dancing together had a uniformed partner.

I used to stay and watch for about an hour. I liked the music, and had to reluctantly admit that the band were superior to my first ever musical heroes, the old Salvation Army band from Ashley Road. The drummer wasn't as good as the Salvation Army drummer though, and he didn't have a big black, bushy moustache.

I told mum about the American Army Band, and she wasn't at all happy that I had gone to College Green alone. She didn't often smack me, but that night she did. We made friends quickly though; she chased me around the room and gave me the raspberry kisses on my neck, and then made me my very own musical instrument. It was only a comb with some thin tissue paper wrapped around it, but she showed me how to play it, and it made a noise like a real instrument. I took it straight up to my room and played it for hours. I shouted "One, two –One, two, three, four" and I played 'In the mood' I played it over and over again. I played it until blowing that comb made my lips tingle, and it made my nose itch. I had more fun playing that comb and paper than I was getting from singing in the choir. I was the smallest and the youngest choir boy by far and always seemed to get shuffled to the back of every queue. When Mr. Fiando asked for volunteers for soloist spots, I raised my hand, and pushed myself forward, but I wasn't asked to sing. I decided to leave, but I wasn't going before Christmas.

Mum was right about the tide turning in the war. Alvar Lidell brought us good news at last as he read the nine o'clock that night. The second Battle of El Alamein had ended, and the German forces under Erwin Rommel had been forced to retreat during the night. All the convoys had reached Malta from Alexandria; Alvar said that an official announcement had been made proclaiming that the island had been "relieved of its siege". I wondered how many German ships and submarines my father had sunk.

I sat munching on a piece of bread and raspberry jam as I listened to Mr. Churchill giving one of his rousing speeches.

"Now this is not the end.
It is not even the beginning of the end.
But it is, perhaps,
The end of the beginning."

It all sounded very complicated, and I couldn't quite understand it, but it was certainly rousing. Mum said he was a bloody Tory, and that Dad didn't like him. I didn't care what Dad thought, I liked Mr. Churchill; he was winning the war for us now.

It was Christmas and I completed my final choir duties. I badly wanted my shilling piece, and once I had it I intended to just walk away. I wouldn't say anything to anyone, I just wouldn't go back. I would return instead to my old place, which was seated behind Rosie Tedesco. I would sit and bellow out my version of Ave Maria, and shout 'Amen' loudly at the appropriate time. I accepted my shilling from Father Doyle, but sadly, that shilling piece wasn't to last for very long.

"Easy come, Easy go," Mum used to say, and so it was with my shilling piece.

I had been nagging Mum for ages to buy me some marbles. I used to stand and watch the boys playing marbles in the playground at school. It all looked very simple, and I knew I would be good at it. All I needed were some marbles to give me a start. Mum kept promising me she would buy some, but she never delivered. There was a bigger boy in the choir, named Leonard. He had a big bag, which was full of marbles. We had, several times, discussed the possibility of my buying some of them, and as we trooped out of the church that night, with my shilling piece burning a hole in my pocket, he offered me a dozen for six pence. I bought them, and he then challenged me to a game. I accepted the challenge, and we started our duel in the gathering gloom outside of the church. We played in the cobblestoned gutter, and my dozen marbles didn't take long to find their way back into his bag. There was more to the game than I had imagined. Leonard offered me another dozen, I gave him my last six pence, and the second dozen rapidly went the same way.

It was a sadder, but wiser young boy who trudged slowly up Zed Alley that night. I normally took those steps two or three at a time, but that night it was a long, slow climb. I think the Devil must have been out to play that night, because as I reached the top of the steps, a man with curly ginger hair stepped out of the darkness and asked me if I wanted to earn a shilling. Mum had trained me for such a moment. I stared straight at him, and then shouted very loudly "Do you think I was born yesterday?" He ran off one way, and I ran the other. I ran all the way home.

I told Mum that I hadn't been paid for being in the choir. I didn't like lying, and I felt guilty, I was beginning to build up a long list of sins ahead of my first confession, and I had been forced to accept that I didn't have what it took to become a saint. I decided I would become a footballer instead.

"Don't worry about it; I will speak to Father Doyle." Mum smiled, but I was no longer smiling. I was worried now, and five minutes later, I made a full confession. Mum smacked me, I cried, and Mum cuddled me up and then taught me another naughty poem. It was called; there was a young lady from Lancs.

Christmas came and went, and it was becoming very cold. With our coal fire blazing, it was much warmer than it had been in the tunnel. Mum bought me a lot of marbles, and she bought Mary a new doll. We had a chicken for Christmas dinner. I had never tasted chicken before. It was even nicer than a pig's trotter. The last of the home made raspberry jam had been eaten It was now one of my favourite things in the world. I did return to the bombed out house at the top of the hill, but the raspberries had all gone. Mum explained the seasons of the year to me. I was tempted to tell her about the biscuit tin and the money but I decided against it. I didn't fancy living on bread and water.

Mum was going out to a party with Mrs. Reilly, who lived down the hill. A lady on the radio had asked all British women to 'make do and mend'. Mum had been without stockings and make up for ages. The lady on the radio had told us how to deal with this problem. Mum listened, and then painted her legs with watered down gravy browning, and asked me to draw some lines down the back of them with her eye brow pencil.

"It will look as if I am wearing stockings." She said

I wasn't very good at drawing the straight lines, and in the end, Mum had to do it herself. We all had a good laugh as she had to get into some very strange positions to do it. She ended up lying on the floor with a mirror in one hand, and the pencil in the other, but the end result was very good.

"Let's hope it doesn't rain" Mum and Mrs. Reilly were giggling as they left the house; they both had gravy browning on their legs.

Mrs. Reilly's husband was away somewhere, he was in the Army. She had two older children, Patsy and David, and Mum asked me if Mary and I would prefer to stay with them for the night. I pointed out to Mum that I was the 'man of the house' and I was perfectly capable of looking after my sister. As soon as Mum had gone, I packed Mary off to bed, piled some coal onto the fire, and curled up in the armchair to listen to the radio. I had a new favourite character in ITMA. His name was Colonel Humphrey Chinstrap, and his catchphrase was, "I don't mind if I do, sir." He was very clever with it and would suddenly appear with the catchphrase whenever anything drink related was mentioned. I sat, listening intently, determined to guess when it was coming.

"Come along boys, hurry up" Tommy Handley was belting out the instructions, "Chop, chop, at the double."

"Did you mention a double? I don't mind if I do, sir." I joined in the laughter and the applause from the Studio audience, as Colonel Chinstrap arrived, but I was slightly annoyed, I hadn't spotted the catchphrase coming again.

There was more good news from Alvar Lidell at nine o'clock.

In the Battle of the Barents Sea, we had won a strategic victory, leading Hitler to largely abandon the use of surface raiders in favour of U boats, Rommel was trapped in Tunisia, the Germans were encircled at Stalingrad, and the Japanese appear ready to abandon Guadalcanal.

"As the year comes to an end, things are looking bright for the Allies." Alvar ended his news broadcast.

I hadn't realised another year was coming to an end. That meant it would be 1943, and I was nearly six. I knelt in front of the fire and prayed that the war would finish shortly; that my father would return home, and that it wouldn't rain on Mum's gravy browned legs.

I must have fallen asleep and I didn't wake up when Mum got home. She must have carried me up to bed. When I came down in the morning, she hadn't risen yet. I noticed there were two unopened packets of American chewing gum on the shelf, and an opened packet of nylon stockings on the table.

Friday 1st January 1943 was a cold and grey day. I took my tennis ball out onto the hill, but the cobblestones were icy and treacherous. It wasn't long before I took a tumble and the ball sped off down the hill. I was an angry young boy that day, with a chip on both shoulders, but I chased after the ball and eventually retrieved it. As I plodded my way back up the slope I slowly calmed down. I was trying hard to understand just why I was so annoyed about the stockings. Part of me felt that I should have been pleased for Mum, but I wasn't; it somehow just didn't quite feel right. I decided not to mention the nylons. Instead, I would express my disapproval by refusing all offers of any chewing gum.

Mum and Mary were both up by the time I returned to the house. Our living room was tiny, compact and sparsely furnished. There was a small table in the bay window, on which my beloved radio and a couple of vases stood; a larger gate leg dining table was positioned against the wall, and there were four matching dining chairs. The solitary armchair took pride of place in front of the fire. It had two wide wooden arms, and brown leather upholstery, which had a multitude of rips and tears from which tufts of the horse hair stuffing was protruding. It had seen better days, but this was my chair; it was just one of the many perks of being the 'man of the house'.

Mary was sitting quietly at the dining table. She was in the process of opening the fourth strip from the first pack of American chewing gum, whilst Mum stood behind her brushing, combing and plaiting her hair. My sister was four now, and had grown into a lovely young girl. She had long dark hair, piercing indigo blue eyes and a shy but ready smile; she was very, very beautiful. She also had a sweet, generous and friendly nature, and was always willing to give me her last toffee or the last chip remaining on her fork. She made friends easily and often, and was forever either sleeping over with, or entertaining one of them at our house. She had a wonderfully simplistic and uncomplicated life style. She would sleep, wake, eat, drink, play and smile. She was forever happy, and the only time I could recall her crying was on the occasion when I had bullied her into being the unwilling partner in my failed knife throwing act. As I entered the room, Mary was just opening the final strip of chewing gum from the first packet. I had to make a decision and I moved smartly to slip the remaining packet into my pocket. I wasn't best pleased with my lack of any will power, but a long day lay ahead, and hunger would never be far away.

Mum explained about New Year and the various customs associated with it. She then taught us the words and the tune of Auld Lang Syne. We then stood together, crossed our arms, held hands and danced in a circle, in front of the fire, as Mum sang the song at the top of her voice.

"Today is New Year day, and now, we will have to make our New Year resolutions. I am the oldest, so I will go first." Mum hesitated but only briefly. "I'm going to cut down on my smoking, and Mary will give me more help with the housework." She turned towards me. "It's Michael's turn now." She looked at me expectantly, but got no response. She smiled and ruffled my hair. I think she knew I liked it when she did that. "Michael will run the errands without complaint, and will stop telling lies."

I didn't argue with her, because I actually enjoyed running the errands. Marlborough Hill was no longer my enemy, but had become more like an old friend. I ran everywhere, and I always counted aloud as I ran. I had a string of personal records. I had a record for every single journey I made. It was '24' to Mr. Smith's fish and chip shop: '26' to The Co-operative Grocery store: '39' to the Off License in Alfred Place and '78' to Parker's Bakery. I had a new, secret hero, and his name was Sydney Wooderson. Wooderson was a famous pre-war British middle distance athlete, and holder of three world records. I had read a lot about him, and I'd watched him running on the grainy images of the Pathe newsreels at the News Theatre in Peter Street. I knew that only injury had deprived him of success at the infamous Berlin Olympics in 1936.

I'd sat in the cinema, enthralled, as I watched the slightly built, bespectacled, balding man turn from an ugly duckling to a graceful swan whenever he donned the running vest of Great Britain. I had already decided that when I grew up, I would become an athlete, and become a world record holder.

The kitchen was the largest room in our house. There was a vast expanse of red flag stoned floor, two gas cookers and a large built in Welsh Dresser, which had lots of shelves. Mum said the second cooker would 'come in handy', if we were ever forced to take in lodgers. I stood at the huge white stone sink as Mum scrubbed my face and neck with the rough piece of toweling.

I had taken Dad's photograph from behind the clock and read his scribbled message on the back. I didn't need Mum to read it out to me now; I was able to read it myself. I looked Mum directly in the eyes. "Do you still love Dad?"

"Of course I do." She replied without hesitation, but the question appeared to trouble her.

I made a face, placed the photograph on top of the opened packet of nylon stockings, and went upstairs to my room. Mum blushed, and hurriedly moved the packet away.

Mum didn't go out that night, and we sat in front of the fire together and I listened to the radio, whilst Mum read a magazine.

"Here comes 'Jerry'." Tommy Handley was at it again. "Just look at the size of that tank; it's a large one."

"Did you say a large one?" Colonel Humphrey Chinstrap appeared to loud applause. "I don't mind if I do, Sir" The studio audience clapped and cheered, and I sat back in my armchair with a contented smile. I had beaten Colonel Chinstrap to it. I had seen it coming, and I'd managed to shout out the phrase before the Colonel had delivered his line.

"Well done." Said Mum, and she ruffled my hair for the second time that day.

Alvar Lidell brought us more good news at nine o'clock. "The Soviet Union announced that 22 German divisions in Stalingrad had been encircled by the Red Army and that 175,000 of the enemy had been killed and 137,650 captured.

"We're winning at last." Mum put down her magazine. She was smiling now.

"Will Dad be coming home soon?"

"It's time for bed." Said Mum, and she had stopped smiling.

I slowly climbed the 39 stairs to my bedroom. I had a feeling that 1943 was going to be a good year.

Mr. Ball was still coughing his way through the night, and the rain water was still dripping into the buckets, but Mr. and Mrs. Muldowney were far less noisy than Skippy and Eileen had been. In fact, there were frequent lengthy periods when I didn't hear them at all. I mentioned this fact to Mum, but she just laughed aloud. "We should be feeling sorry for poor Mr. Muldowney then."

I didn't understand her, and she cuddled me as she chuckled. "One day you will understand, but you must remind me to tell Mrs. Reilly that story."

From time to time, I was still slipping out under cover of darkness to visit Park Street and College Green despite warnings from Mum to keep away from the area. Mum said that there had been big trouble between the black and the white American soldiers. I didn't tell her that I had seen her and Mrs. Reilly walking down Park Street together. Mum was wearing her black fur coat, although she had always told me that women who wore fur coats were probably not wearing any knickers.

I would often run home in the dark, and sometimes, if I was feeling particularly brave, I would run home via Johnny Ball Lane. Johnny Ball Lane led from Lewin's Mead up to Upper Maudlin Street and was a very dark and scary place. More often than not there would be American soldiers in the lane. They were there cuddling up to their sweethearts. They would usually shout at me as I ran past them in the darkness, but I never stopped, and I never looked back until I had reached the top of the lane.

I was going to Mass on a cold Sunday morning in February, and I was walking slowly down Johnny Ball Lane when I found it. The crisp ten shilling note came fluttering in the breeze, out of a doorway and landed right at my feet. I decided it was a miracle sent from heaven, so I skipped Mass, and bought two comics from Mr. Gormley's shop at the bottom of Horfield Road instead. I kept a single six pence coin out of the change, and gave the rest of the money to Mum.

The following day we all headed down to Milk Street. Mum was flushed with excitement as we rummaged around in Madame Bessel's second hand clothes shop. Mum bought a pair of high heeled shoes for herself and a nice red coat for Mary. I had been nagging her for a navy blue raincoat for ages, and Madame Bessel produced one. I heard her telling Mum that apart from a couple of cigarette burns; it was "As good as new." It was several sizes too large for me, but Mum explained that "I would soon grow into it." I wore it home, and I wore it with pride.

On the way home we stopped off at Mr. Walt Eager's pet shop. It was packed with assorted birds and animals and I asked Mum if I could have a puppy for my next birthday present.

"We'll see." She said, but I knew that usually meant 'No'.

"Can I have a parrot instead then?" I was very good at nagging when I put my mind to it. I was reading a book called Treasure Island, and Long John Silver, the pirate in the book, had a parrot. Mr. Eager had several parrots in his shop, and I knew that Mum still had money left over from the ten shilling note. Mum didn't reply, but I saw her whispering with Mr. Eager before we headed off for home.

I went to bed that night and dreamt of raincoats, pirates, puppies and parrots. Mr. Ball was coughing badly, the rain water was dripping steadily into the buckets, and Mr. and Mrs. Muldowney chose that night to be extremely noisy. None of the noises stopped me from drifting off to sleep and dreaming. As I dozed off, I made a mental note to tell Mum about Mr. and Mrs. Muldowney. She would need to tell Mrs. Reilly about it, and I no longer had to feel sorry for Mr. Muldowney.

I had always known that 1943 was going to be a good year, and it had started well.

6 PARROTS AND PUPPIES

The idea of owning a parrot gradually took root in my imagination, and it slowly became more attractive than the prospect of owning a puppy. I read and reread Treasure Island, and really fancied the idea of a parrot named Captain Flint perched on my shoulder whilst it chattered pirate phrases like "Pieces of eight," or "Stand by to go about." I memorized the words of Long John Silver as he described his parrot. 'Now that bird,' Silver would say, 'is, may be, two hundred years old, Hawkins- they live forever mostly, and if anybody's seen more wickedness it must be the devil himself. She's sailed with England- the great Cap'n England, the pirate. She's been at Madagascar, and at Malabar, and Surinam, and Providence, and Portobello ... She was at the boarding of the Viceroy of the Indies out of Goa, she was, and to look at her you would think she was a babby.'

I took to wandering down to Milk Street at every available opportunity. I loitered around Mr. Eager's shop and studied the various birds which were available. Eventually, I made my choice. The chosen parrot was grey, and had huge wings and an even bigger beak. Having made my selection, I started to drop hints to my mother as my birthday grew closer, and ever so slowly, she started to weaken.

It was just after Easter when I had the appointment at Tower Hill Clinic for an x ray examination. Mum stressed to everyone who was prepared to listen, that it was purely a routine check-up following my 'pneumonia' illness. Mum was due to pick me up from school, but she was late. Miss Lynch kindly stayed on to look after me until Mum arrived. She had a little chat with me about Charles Dickens and David Copperfield. This was the book that we were studying at school, and Miss Lynch was keen to talk about Miss Peggoty and her relationship with David Copperfield. I loved Miss Lynch with her soft and gentle Irish dialect, and I hung on to every word she spoke to me.

"Your mother has done a splendid job with your reading and your writing," She studied me closely, and I could feel a question coming. "Has she ever taught you any poetry?"

I nodded without giving too much thought to the question

"Would you recite some of it for me please?"

The panic started slowly. It started initially in my knees, but quickly travelled straight to my brain which immediately ceased to function normally. The problem was that There was young lady from Ealing, There was a young lady from Hitchen and There was a young lady from Lancs., were the only poems Mum had ever taught me, and I was well aware that they were all unsuitable examples of poems for me to recite to Miss Lynch. Then, just as all seemed lost, from somewhere in the deepest recesses of my memory came inspiration. I remembered those magical nights when we were living at Long Ashton. Those nights when Mary and I would sit cross legged in front of a roaring coal fire whilst Mum told us the stories about her school days. I recalled the look of pride on her face as she performed her party piece and recited every single verse of the Song of Hiawatha. I didn't know every single verse, but I was able to remember just a few lines. I closed my eyes and tried to conjure up a picture the scene. Suddenly I could see it all very clearly. I could see Mum standing there, and just as she had done on that far off night, I held my hands together as if in prayer, took a deep breath and started.

"The song of Hiawatha,
By Henry Wadsworth Longfellow.
By the shores of Gitche Gumee, by the shining Big-Sea-Water,
Stood the wigwam of Nokomis, daughter of the Moon, Nokomis.
Dark behind it rose the forest, rose the black and gloomy pine-trees,
Rose the firs with cones upon them; bright before it beat the water,
Beat the clear and sunny water; beat the shining Big-Sea-Water."

That was as much as I could remember, but it was enough. I opened my eyes and Miss Lynch had tears in her eyes. She took a handkerchief from the sleeve of her jumper and dabbed away the tears.

"I knew it; I just knew it," She was smiling now. "What a wonderful, educated and cultured lady your mother must be."

She rummaged around in her desk and pulled out a small book. It was bound in blue leather, with a gold inscription on the front. She held it out in front of her.

"A book is the fount of all knowledge, Michael, and this little book is the source that feeds the fount. I want you to have it; I want you to use it, and I want you to use it wisely. It will open many doors for you." She placed the book in my hand. "It's a dictionary, and inside you will find every word in the English language you will ever need."

When Mum eventually arrived we were very late, and Mum couldn't stay to chat, although Miss Lynch wanted to. I showed Mum my new dictionary, and told her what Miss Lynch had said.

"I've never been called 'educated and cultured' before. Thanks for the warning. That's a lot to live up to." Mum appeared to be in a good mood, so I didn't tell her how close I had been to reciting 'There was a young lady from Ealing.'

It was quite a rush getting to Tower Hill, but we made it and the Doctor came back with good news.

"All the old lesions have healed, and there are no sign of any new ones."

We headed home down Carey's Lane, turned off along Ellbroad Street and celebrated the good news by buying a portion of fish and chips, and a portion of faggots and chips from Mr. Di Stefano's shop. I had the faggots and they were delicious. I made a mental note to add 'faggots' to my list of favourite things in the whole wide world.

We didn't have a care in the world that night as Mum held my hand and we strolled home together. I made sure that we went home along Milk Street, and as we passed Walt Eager's shop, I told her about Long John Silver and his parrot Captain Flint.

"Pieces of Eight," I squawked as we looked at the birds in the window. Mum ruffled my hair, and I knew that I would be getting Captain Flint for my birthday present.

It didn't take me long to realise I had made a mistake. Captain Flint didn't appear to like me, and he certainly wasn't going to talk for me. I spent hours with him. I spent entire days, and long, lonely weeks. Night after night, I sat with him repeating the phrase "Pieces of Eight," Captain Flint sat on his perch staring straight at me with those beady eyes, but he remained silent.

"I don't think he likes me," I was hoping against hope that Mum might return him, or maybe swap him for a puppy, but she was unsympathetic. "He won't talk for me."

"Let me try," Mum was keen to take over, but she had no more success than I had. Night after night, and day after day, she sat and spoke with the parrot, but Captain Flint remained silent.

"That bird is a waste of good money." Mum was not amused.

"Oremus," Father Doyle stood in front of the fire and opened up his arms. "Let us pray."

"Amen" Mum had confided in me that whenever she didn't know a response in Latin, and I was unable to assist her, she would just say 'Amen.'

We all prayed together, but we were rushing through it; we were all in a hurry. Mum was going out with Mrs. Reilly again. I was anxious to read my new dictionary or any one of the many books I had now acquired, and Mary couldn't wait to get to her bed.

We were all on our knees praying, but I was feeling uneasy. I was very conscious that Captain Flint was standing on his perch, shifting around from one foot to the other, whilst studying me closely.

"In nomine Patris, et Filii…" Father Doyle was in the middle of making his sign of the cross when Mum interrupted him.

"Amen." She blurted the word out. I knew it was the right word, but I knew she was saying it at the wrong time.

"You came in too early Mrs. Kelly." Father Doyle scowled at Mum, before starting again. "In nomine Patris, et Filii et Spiritus Sancti." He then paused before nodding encouragingly in Mum's direction.

"Amen." said Mum, and Father Doyle nodded again, but this time he nodded approvingly.

"There was a young lady from Ealing," From nowhere, the parrot had decided to join in the conversation. He spoke the words with total and absolute clarity, and in a voice that unquestionably belonged to my mother.

The room fell silent. Father Doyle looked shocked and stood stock still, staring open mouthed at Mum. Mum, in turn, stood still and stared open mouthed at the parrot. The parrot, however, had eyes for me and me alone. He fixed me with a steely, unblinking gaze. It was at that very moment that I knew, without any shadow of doubt, that the parrot really disliked me, and I also knew that the feeling was mutual.

"I'm sorry Father Doyle, he's a new pet, and we certainly haven't taught him anything like that," said Mum rather lamely.

"Dominus vobiscum," Father Doyle ignored Mum and started again.

"Et cum spiritu tuo," replied Mum. She sounded like a proper Catholic and I wanted to applaud.

"She could piddle all over the ceiling," There was no stopping Captain Flint now, and once again, he spoke the words with total clarity, and this time he sounded exactly like Mum.

Mum leapt up quickly and covered the cage with a large red blanket. The parrot fell silent, and I felt a huge sense of relief, because I knew the next three lines, and I knew the language was about to get even worse.

"That is a most inappropriate pet for you to have with two young children in the house, Mrs. Kelly," I heard Father Doyle rebuking Mum as she led him down the hallway to the front door."

Captain Flint was returned to Mr. Eager's shop early the next day. Mum was unable to get a refund of her money, but she returned home with a surprise for me.

I firmly believe that we start the painful process of growing up when we reach the age of reason, and that we reach the age of reason as soon as we develop a conscience. Unfortunately, with a conscience comes guilt, and guilt is one of the most powerful and destructive of our emotions. I experienced guilt for the very first time on that sunny day in late June 1943. Mum had been very grumpy all morning, and she went on and on and on about the parrot. She was moaning about the money she had spent on it, and groaning about the embarrassment it had caused her with Father Doyle. She told me that

I had to learn the difference between needing and wanting. Suddenly, completely out of the blue, I found myself swamped with guilt as my brain accepted that I had bullied and manipulated Mum into that expensive and wasted purchase. I suppose at that stage I should have apologized, but my short temper took me in a different direction and I went on the attack. I shouted at her about her nights out with Mrs. Reilly, and I challenged her about talking to the American soldiers. Initially she looked shocked and was silent, but then she fell into the most awful rage; screamed at me, took me by the shoulders and shook me.

"How dare you, you little monster." She threw me onto the bed and smacked my thighs with the back of her hair brush. This was always her punishment of choice when I'd pushed her too far,

But as was usual when we fought, we ended up crying in each other's arms, with Mum showering my neck with her raspberry kisses, and with both of us saying 'sorry'.

I lay in her arms with my head on her shoulder and her face was against mine. She was crying, and not for the first time, I tasted the salt of her tears.

"I wish you were older Michael, and maybe then you would understand." She sighed and pulled me even closer. "I'd only known your father for a short time when this bloody war started, and he's now been away for another four years. I'm not even sure I would recognize him if he walked through the door." She fell into a thoughtful silence before she continued. "I'm tired Michael; tired of lying in bed every night and worrying about you and Mary; tired of waiting every day for the telegram boy to knock on the door with his bad news about your father; tired of worrying where the next penny and the next meals are coming from; and I'm tired of being alone. Surely you don't begrudge me some adult company with a little happiness, however shallow and fleeting it may be. I'm growing old, I'm growing old fast, and I'm growing old alone. Please don't judge me until you are much older."

I didn't answer, because I didn't really understand, but the lack of understanding didn't stop me from feeling guilty again.

"I'm taking that bloody parrot back today." Mum was sitting on her bed with both feet in a bowl of warm soapy water. She was wearing a pale blue petticoat, and I could clearly see her underwear beneath it. She had hoisted the petticoat up above her knees and had covered her thighs with a large white towel which she had folded across her lap. She reached down and cupping her hands together, scooped the water on to her legs, before scrubbing them vigorously with a small piece of grey pumice stone. The scrubbing continued for some time before she was satisfied, and then she stood up, and carefully dried her legs with the towel. She ran her hands up and down each leg, softly caressing the pink, shiny skin, and then nodded in self approval.

"As smooth as a baby's bum," she declared with a smile as she rummaged around in the top drawer of the dressing table. She produced a pair of nylon stockings and I watched in fascinated silence as she carefully placed a foot into each stocking, and then slowly and lovingly eased and smoothed her legs into them.

Throughout all this, Mary had been sitting quietly at the dressing table, staring into the mirror whilst pretending to apply make up to her face. Mum now lifted her from the stool and placed her on the bed alongside me.

"I doubt that I will get any money back, but I will give it a good go." Mum leant forward, her nose almost touching the mirror and studied her reflection intently. She frowned, pursed her lips and placed both hands on her cheeks, and pulled gently at the skin around her eyes.

"Am I looking older?" It was more of an observation than a question so I didn't bother to reply, and I decided not to mention the solitary strand of grey hair I had noticed at the back of her head.

She was ready to prepare her face now. Make up had been in short supply in those early years of the war. 'Make do and mend,' the man on the radio was constantly telling us and Mum did just that. Shortages and rationing meant that she had to use crushed beetroot juice to add colouring to her lips, and she made do with a small piece of burnt cork for her eyes, but times had changed, and things were different now that the Yanks were in town. The beetroot juice and the burnt cork still sat on the dressing table, but had been joined by lipsticks, face powder, a pink powder puff, mascara, eye shadow and a large cut glass bottle of perfume. There was a pink rubber ball attached to the perfume bottle, which when squeezed, produced a powerful spray of the sweet smelling perfume.

Mum pouted her lips and expertly painted on the bright red

lipstick; already, she was beginning to look like a film star. She rolled her lips together and ran the tip of her middle finger over her teeth. She was almost done now. All that remained was a quick session with the powder puff.

"No point in messing around with my eyes," she joked, "Mr. Eager never looks that high."

It didn't take her long to select a dress. Her choice was the shot silk tight fitting one, and as she pirouetted in front of the mirror, I marveled at the way the dress changed colour from blue to pink, and then to purple. Mum tugged at the dress around her breast and her bottom until she was happy with the look.

"I'm ready for battle." She smiled and I felt sorry for Mr. Eager, because I knew that Mum usually won her battles.

I felt another pang of guilt as I watched Mum struggling down the hill. The parrot's cage was enormous, and she was unable to get a decent grip on it. From beneath the red blanket I could hear the muffled squawks of protest from Captain Flint, but I felt no sympathy for him. Mum had said. 'We've given him his golden chances, and he's let them pass him by'. I felt the same way.

I needn't have worried about Mum and the cage. She was less than halfway down the hill when Mr. Jones appeared from his front garden. He and Mum exchanged a few words and then Mr. Jones took the cage from her and they marched off down Whitson Street together. When Mum needed a knight in shining armour, one always seemed to appear.

It was several hours before she returned and I spotted her huffing and puffing her way back up the hill. The parrot's cage was gone, but she was cradling something in her arms. At first I thought she was bringing a baby home. She actually was, but as she drew closer I could see it was a baby dog. I ran down the hill to meet them.

Mum took the puppy from under her coat and thrust him into my arms. "There you are. You wanted a bloody dog, so there you go; now you have one. He's your responsibility; yours to look after...Happy Birthday."

I clutched the tiny dog to my chest. He was trembling and I could feel his heart fluttering against my shirt. I lowered my face and placed my cheek against his head. The puppy looked up, startled, studied me closely for several seconds, and then gently started to lick my face. Like all the good love stories, it started with a kiss.

My new puppy was tiny, chubby, and was snow white, apart from a black spot around his right eye. I named him Beppo, which was the same name as a clown who featured in a comic I was currently reading. We both had a lot to learn, but we learnt quickly, and we learnt from one another. I taught him to climb the thirty nine stairs which led from the hallway to our bedroom, and he, eventually, taught himself to come back down. Most importantly, he taught me how to love unconditionally. I had previously spent much of my life scrounging as much food as I could from other peoples' plates. Now I found myself feeding another living being from my own plate. What was more, I was enjoying doing it. Hour by hour, day by day, the boy and his dog had grown closer until they had become as one.

The weeks slipped by and we were soon enjoying the long, sun filled days of the school summer holidays. Back in those days, a dog would roam free, wearing neither leash nor collar, and Beppo used to join me wherever I went. Mum was invariably taking Mary to work with her, and we were left to fend for ourselves. We wandered happily around Bristol exploring the highways and byways, the parks and the many bombed building sites. Life was one long adventure, but summer was fading and the holiday was drawing to an end.

Mum had left me with a long list of chores, and I got the first one out of the way quickly, but it didn't go well. I left Beppo at home and made the walk of shame down to Mr. Keeler's pawn shop. All we had left to pawn were some sheets and blankets, and I carried them in two bundles, one under each arm. Mum had made it clear that we needed two shillings and sixpence from Mr. Keeler, but after closely examining the bedding with his eye piece, he gave me just two shillings. I didn't argue and trudged back up the hill feeling totally inadequate.

Beppo waddled up the hill with me for our second task. With the two shilling piece safely tucked away in my pocket, I carried the ration book and a note from Mum to Mr. Morris. I knew there were no coupons left in the book, but I no longer worried about that aspect, I had done it on many occasions now, and knew the score. Mum's note requested two ounces of margarine and a similar quantity of cheese. Beppo settled down outside and I joined the usual queue of women at Mr. Morris's position. He was his usual bubbly self, whistling his happy tunes, and smiling and joking with the ladies, but he turned serious as I came to the head of the queue. He read Mum's note, and rubbed his chin in a thoughtful silence. He leant forward, beckoned me towards him and then spoke to me in a quiet voice.

"Tell your mother," His voice dropped to a whisper, "Tell her that stocks are low. I can only do favours for regular customers, and I haven't seen her for ages. Have you got that?" I nodded and he took his thin piece of wire and sliced off the tiniest of slivers from the giant slabs of cheese and margarine. My two shilling piece and the order shot across the overhead wire to the cashier and then came shooting back. Mr. Morris handed me my change, the receipt and the food. He tapped his nose,

"Regular" he repeated.

Beppo and I headed for home, but we were hungry, and I was about to demolish the scant rations when I had a brainwave. We had much more change than I had expected, so we set off back up the hill. Our destination was Mr. Smith's chip shop and our prize was a large bag of chips. Beppo sat in the doorway in his usual way, his head on one side, and his eyes fixed on Mr. Smith, but Mr. Smith didn't throw him the usual spare chips. Instead, we had a bonus. Mr. Smith handed me a present for the dog; he gave Beppo his very own bag of chips.

We headed across the road and squeezed through the green door into our secret garden. The grass was waist high now, but we muscled our way through it to reach the garden bench. The raspberries and the gooseberries were long gone, but the two of blackbirds who had been feasting on them were still there. We sat munching away on our chips as I told Beppo some stories. I told him about the blitz and the tunnel. I told him about the various people who had flittered in and out of my life. I told him about Mr. Brown, Mr. Lloyd, Jacob, I had got as far as Nurse Pamela when I realized that Beppo was asleep. I carried him home and he was still asleep when Mum and Mary came in.

Mum was fine about the money and the food. I told her what Mr. Morris had said. She made a face. "Dirty old bugger. I would rather starve."

The holiday was almost over; it was almost time to return to school. I was worried how Beppo would cope with it. Mum tried to reassure me that everything would be alright, but I still worried.

I was right to be worried, because Beppo fretted when I returned to school. He stood on the corner whining as I left in the morning, and would be in the same spot waiting for me when I returned in the afternoon. As soon as I appeared he would come charging down the hill to greet me.

I missed him as much as he missed me, but we always made up for it in the evenings, especially when Mum went out with Mrs. Reilly. With the aid of the dictionary that Miss Lynch had given me, I was reading constantly, and I would curl up in my armchair, alternately reading or listening to the radio. Beppo was always there on my lap, snuggled up and snoring contentedly.

I was reading three books around that time. A book about Sydney Wooderson, my favourite athlete; 'Anchors Aweigh', a book about Lieutenant Ian Fairbairn, a dashing Royal Navy Officer who was sinking lots of German submarines in the North Atlantic, and 'Goddard of the Yard', a detective book about Inspector Donald Goddard. I felt very guilty about Goddard, because, after all these years, he had usurped Paul Temple as my favourite detective. Goddard,' a tall, bluff spoken man from Barnsley', was a completely different personality than Temple. He didn't say 'By Timothy', when he came across a clue, he always whispered 'Ay oop lad'. In the latest chapter I had read, Goddard had described good detective work as being 80% observation, 5% deduction and 15% luck. I knew I had to do more observations.

It was November, and Mum said it was five months since she had brought the dog home for me, but that night he wasn't waiting on the corner when I came home from school. Mum was beside herself with worry.

"I was hoping he was with you."

I searched high and low. I knocked on every door, I searched the secret garden in the dark, I asked Mr. Smith, but nobody had seen him. I found him the following morning. He was curled up asleep in the coal house, his head in the upturned saucer, only he wasn't asleep, he was dead. Mum said the saucer had been full of rat poison, and that someone must have left the door of the coal house open. I didn't cry. I just felt sad and empty. Mum said we would give him a good Catholic send off. She dug a hole in the back garden, and I knelt on the damp grass with Mary by my side. Our heads were bowed and our hands were clasped together.

"Oremus," said Mum, opening her arms wide just as Father Doyle did. "Let us pray," and we prayed. Mum then told us a story about a little boy who had rescued a puppy and had brought love and happiness into the puppy's life. The puppy was in heaven now, but he wanted to say thank you to the little boy. He wanted the boy to be happy with all of the memories.

I dreamt of Beppo that night. He was sitting in the doorway of Mr. Smith's shop. His head was on one side and he was gazing intently at Mr. Smith who threw him a chip.

I woke up and fumbled around on my blanket, seeking his wet nose. I didn't find it of course. Like all the greatest love stories it had started with a kiss, but had ended with a broken heart.

7 FOOTBALL AND FAMILY

Mum told me that time mended everything, and that included broken hearts. "Believe me, Michael, I'm speaking from experience, I know," she said, and she was wearing a very sad face. I did believe her implicitly, because Mum was almost always right, and sure enough, by the time another Christmas had come and gone, my own broken heart had healed.

Christmas in 1943 was very good; the best I could remember. We made our own Christmas trimmings that year. We cut up some little pieces of coloured paper and Mum made some glue using flour and water. We spent hours pasting the pieces of paper together, and then Mum stood on a chair to hang them around the room. She was wobbling rather precariously on that chair, and she made me cling on to her ankles to prevent her from falling. We laughed until our stomachs ached. It had been a long time since we had laughed like that and it felt good.

I don't know from where or how she had obtained it, but Mum produced a large tin of Spam. We ate it all along with some fried potatoes, and after we had eaten a huge meal we sang some Christmas carols. We normally had just a few nuts and some oranges in our Christmas stockings, but that year we had real presents. Mum had bought Mary two knitting needles, and together Mum and I had unravelled two old woollen cardigans. I stood with my arms in the air whilst Mum wound the wool around my thumbs, before winding it back off again and making it into four large balls. Mary was delighted with her present, and so was I with mine. Mum had bought me a brand new toy Tommy gun from the Milliners shop at the top of Sussex Place. It was painted red, and had a bright yellow handle on one side. When I turned the handle quickly, a cog travelled across a piece of metal and created a rattling noise that sounded just like a real gun. All I needed now were some friends to play 'soldiers' with.

'No man is an island; no man can stand alone.' This was a line from the book Anchors Aweigh, which I was currently reading. I loved the sound of that line, but I didn't fully understand what it meant. I asked Mum for help, and she explained it to me. She told me how from time to time all of us encountered problems in our lives. She then made clear why dealing with those problems was so much easier if we had a friend to stand by our side and help us. I reflected on all this as I lay in bed that night. I understood now why Mum had Mrs. Reilly to help her, and why my sister, Mary, was developing an ever increasing circle of friends. I was forced to accept that I had nobody to turn to, and I knew right away that I had to do something about it. I resolved there and then that I would now find a friend.

The following morning I rose early and set off in search of friendship. I took my new gun with me as I had a hunch that it could be a passport to popularity. Trouble doesn't travel up a hill. I decided to ignore Mum's warning, and headed off down the hill. It was just as if fate was guiding my footsteps, because I'd travelled no further than fifty yards when I came across a group of five boys. They were playing, and they were playing 'soldiers'. I stood and studied the two rival armies. On my left was Ronny Pascoe. Ronny was on his stomach, crawling through the undergrowth of his front garden. From time to time, he paused and fired a volley of imaginary shots from a make belief rifle. The two boys crawling behind him were complete strangers and Ronny was very much in control. With a wave of his hand, he signalled his troops to advance and they always obeyed him. I felt as if I was at the cinema watching a film.

Across the road, at the far end of Cleveland Road, I could just see the Carnavale brothers, Peter and Dennis. They were crouching behind a wall at the front of their house, occasionally popping their heads over the parapet to fire an imaginary machine gun at the enemy. Something deep inside told me that this was my moment; my time to impress. I casually stepped forward and aimed my gun in the direction of the Carnavale brothers. Turning the handle of my

Tommy gun at speed I fired at them for what felt like an eternity. I stopped and waited for a reaction. The Carnavale brothers stayed behind the safety of their wall, but Ronny and his army came marching out to greet me.

I knew Ronny only vaguely, we had never actually spoken. My mother often used to stop and speak with Aggie, Ronny's mother, whenever we passed each other on the hill, but Ronny and I always kept our distance, eying each other with caution. Now we were alone and face to face. Ronny was a big boy, with a large round face, a severe fringe and a permanently runny nose. I also suffered from a runny nose, but Ronny's nose was in a different league to mine. I studied him now, and watched the thick stream of bright yellow snot sliding down towards his upper lip. He sniffed loudly, and he sniffed just in time. If I had been expecting any gratitude, it wasn't forthcoming.

"What do you think you are doing?" He snapped. "And what's that?" He snatched my gun from my grasp, and studied it closely. His troops shuffled forward menacingly and took their place by his side. I realised I had chosen the wrong side, and I was in trouble. I began to feel uncomfortable, and I stole a glance along the road towards the Carnavale brothers, but no help was forthcoming from them. They remained firmly entrenched behind their wall, and I didn't blame them.

Ronny sniffed, and once again his timing was impeccable.

"That's not a proper gun." He maintained eye contact as he cold bloodedly smashed my beloved gun against his front garden wall. My gun splintered into several pieces, and the all-important strip of metal became detached and clanked forlornly into the gutter. Ronny moved closer still, and his troops moved with him. I didn't back off, but I prepared myself to flee.

"You are now my prisoner," He sniffed again; "I will have to torture you, and then probably kill you later." I decided that now was the right time to back off and now was also the right time to flee; I decided not to hang around and I ran off down the hill at full speed and without looking back. My first venture into friendship had failed miserably.

I didn't slow down until I had almost reached Eugene Street. Then I stopped dead in my tracks as I heard that most magical of sounds; the sound of happy children at play. I turned the corner and my heart skipped a beat. There they were, right in front of me. At the far end of the road I could see about a dozen young girls of roughly my age. They were hopping, skipping, jumping, playing ball with one another and chanting.

"Plainsy, clapsy, round the world and backsy," chanted the tall, slender girl with pig tails as she multitasked with a tennis ball against the wall. She was throwing it, catching it, whilst at the same time twirling and chanting

"One, two, three, my mother caught a flea; she put it in the teapot and made a cup of tea. The flea jumped out, my mother gave a shout and in came daddy with his shirt hanging out." chanted the tiny, olive skinned girl with black ringlets and large brass hooped ear rings.

But the girls at play were not uppermost in my thoughts. The bulk of the street was taken up by a large group of boys who were engaged in a fast, furious and frantic game of football. It was a good game as well, and looked to be of a high standard. The tennis ball was pinging around off the cobblestones, the concrete pavements and the brick walls at lightning speed. There was passing, dribbling, shooting, ferocious tackling, a lot of shouting and quite a lot of swearing. I desperately wanted to play; I wanted a piece of the action.

I stood behind the goalmouth at the Marlborough Hill end. The goalmouth was defined by a tree and a large brick pillar. The goalkeeper looked and sounded as if he was the 'Boss'. He was snarling and barking out orders and instructions to all and sundry. He was a stocky lad with a barrel chest and a shock of thick brown hair. He looked the part, and was even wearing a green crew necked jumper and a pair of woollen gloves, that was the trademark uniform of the professional pre-war goalkeepers whose photos I had seen on the backs of the cigarette cards which were all the rage back then.

I moved in closer, hoping for an invitation to join in, but no invitation was forthcoming so I just watched whilst fielding and retrieving a few stray shots that flew wide of their marks. The 'boss' and the fresh faced, blonde boy with slightly protruding teeth were bickering and arguing like an old married couple.

"Don't fart about with it back there John. Just get your foot through it and clear it." Snapped the 'Boss' as another shot had just missed its target.

"That was your ball Pat; you should have come for it." John clearly wasn't frightened to fight his corner.

"Our John's right," A smaller, younger mirror image of the blonde boy spoke up.

"Keep out of this Frank," John waved his finger at the younger boy. "I can sort it out myself, thank you."

"Freddy: Your dinner is getting cold." The loud cry came from an upstairs window of the block of flats. I could see the dark haired lady leaning out of the window.

Freddy turned out to be the chubby lad in grossly oversized wellington boots, who had not really played any real part in the game so far. He shrugged his shoulders apologetically to the 'Boss' and headed rapidly and enthusiastically towards his food.

"That's all we bloody needed," said the 'Boss', and then he paused, slowly turned and stared at me. "Do you want a game?"

Did I want a game? Did I want a game? I almost passed out with excitement as I nodded my response.

"What's your name?" The 'Boss' asked me with a smile.

"Mike," I nervously stepped on to the playing area.

The boss cupped his hands around his mouth. "We've got Mike," he bellowed, and turned to face me. "We're three- two down. Get up front and sort it out."

It didn't take long to sort it out. A big boy wearing long, brown gabardine trousers quickly scored an equalizer, and then came my big chance. A long throw out from the 'Boss' took a wicked bounce off of the cobblestones. It was the precise situation which all my practice on the hill had prepared me for. In a flash, I was through on goal, but the ball ran away from me and the goalkeeper raced off his line to challenge me. From the corner of my eye I saw two other defenders converging on me. I was about to become the meat in a painful sandwich, but I closed my eyes and just got my toe to the ball a split second before the three defenders hit me. I was in a lot of pain as I lay there and watched in what felt like slow motion as the ball trickled over the line. My teammates rushed to congratulate me, and the 'Boss' grabbed the ball and stuffed into his pocket. He then placed the index finger and the thumb of his left hand into his mouth and let out a piercing whistle.

"That's it; full time, we won four–three." He waved away the protests from the opposition, tapping an imaginary watch on his wrist. "It is full time," he insisted and waved them away. Slowly they all dispersed in their various grumbling little groups. He really was the

'Boss'.

Johnny, Frank and the 'Boss' sat on the pavement with their backs to the brick wall, staring out across the wasteland of bricks and rubble that was the other side of Eugene Street in 1943. The 'Boss' beckoned me to join them. I did with pounding heart. For the first time in my life I felt a part of something special. I was no longer an island.

The 'Boss' eventually broke the silence. "Good goal Mike." Johnny and Frank nodded and added their muttered congratulations. The 'Boss' stood up and stretched. "Where do you live?"

I waved vaguely in the direction of Marlborough Hill. "Up the hill."

"What's your second name?"

"Kelly," I replied. I was trying hard to sound casual.

"Fuck me," the 'Boss' suddenly looked as if he had seen a ghost. "Are you Joe Kelly's boy?" I nodded. The 'boss' shook his head in obvious astonishment. "I'm Pat, your bloody cousin…I'm Frank's boy; Frank is Joe's brother," he continued as I remained silent. I didn't know what to say. Mum had never told me any of this. I didn't know that I had a cousin or an Uncle.

My newly found cousin extended his hand and shook mine warmly. "Have you been to see Granny Kelly yet?" he continued. I shook my head; it was news to me that I had a Granny.

"Come on down again tomorrow and I'll take you over to see her. She's always talking about you."

I said goodbye to my new friends and ran home in a daze. I had wings on my heels as I ran back up the hill that day. I couldn't wait to tell Mum about my adventure. In one foul swoop I had discovered football, friends and family.

It took a lot to render my mother speechless, but I managed to achieve it on that cold, grey afternoon in late December 1943. Mum was relaxed and in high spirits when I first arrived home. She was upstairs in her bedroom; sitting at the dressing table, and preparing herself for another night out with Mrs. Reilly. She looked almost ready. The nylon stockings were on, her make-up looked complete, and her hair was shining from what had clearly been a good brushing. She was sitting there, fully dressed and quietly sipping a cup of tea.

She was only listening with half an ear as I started to blurt out my story of the day's adventure, but she quickly looked up and took notice when I mentioned Paddy, Uncle Frank and Granny Kelly.

"Hold on; hold on; slow down," she placed her hands in the air; palms facing towards me and signalled for me to calm down.

"Now start again," she said, "and take your time. "I took a deep breath and started all over. Now, she was paying full attention. She was hanging on to my every word, and when I'd finished, she fell silent, and she sat staring into space. She was looking worried, anxious and thoughtful.

I wondered for a moment what I had done wrong, and I stood waiting for a reaction or an explanation. Eventually she spoke. "Are you saying that you really intend to visit Granny Kelly?"

It felt like a bit of a silly question, but I answered it. "Yes, I'm going tomorrow. Paddy's taking me over to meet her. He said she's always talking about me."

Mum didn't reply immediately. She took a cigarette from the packet on the dressing table, lit it, and took a couple of deep puffs. She then blew two magnificent smoke rings, and we both studied them closely as they rose into the air and swirled around the room. We watched them until they slowly disintegrated and disappeared. I was so desperate to grow up and blow smoke rings like my mother did. She was very, very good at it.

"I want you to promise me just one thing, Michael," I was paying attention now, because Mum was speaking in her serious voice.

"Just promise me you will be careful what you say to her. I would prefer that you didn't mention my nights out with Mrs. Reilly. Do you understand? That old witch has never, ever liked me, and I don't want to give her any ammunition."

'That old witch' I had a brief mental image of Granny Kelly flying through the night on a broomstick, and for just a moment I had second thoughts about my visit, but then I pictured Paddy's face. He would be upset if I failed to show and I wasn't going to disappoint my cousin, Paddy was the 'Boss'. I promised Mum I would be careful, and not let her down. After all, I now considered myself to be a bit of an expert on the interrogation techniques used by women, and I was confident I could always stay one step ahead of them. Granny Kelly wouldn't be getting any information from me.

"Happy New Year," said Mum as she set off for her night out

with Mrs. Reilly. "I've put some coal on the fire, and there's bread and jam in the larder. Look after Mary, and don't stay up too late. Be a good boy, I'll see you in the morning."

I couldn't believe that it was New Year again. It seemed like only yesterday when Mum had gone out with the gravy browning on her legs; when I had sat and listened to Alvar Lidell telling how the Germans were encircled at Stalingrad, and how Rommel was trapped in Tunisia. That following day we had all sat down together and made our New Year resolutions. I was sad when I realised that those resolutions, despite the good intentions, hadn't changed a thing. I was still telling lots of lies, and Mum hadn't cut back on her smoking at all. If anything, she was smoking more. I wondered whether life would always be like that; whether it would always be just one long sequence of broken promises and dreams. I turned on the radio and chose a book to read. It was a toss-up between Goddard of the Yard, Anchors Aweigh, and Sydney Wooderson. Tonight, it was Inspector Goddard's turn.

"Ay oop lad," I whispered as I opened the book at Chapter Ten. Goddard was close to solving yet another crime, and it was all down to 'observation'. I knew that I needed to do some observations.

I read for a few hours, and then listened to the Nine o'clock News on the radio. It felt as if we were winning the war at long last, but Mr. Lidell said it was 'far from over', but he then gave us some good news. The German battleship Scharnhorst had been sunk off North Cape (in the Arctic) by an array of British cruisers and destroyer torpedoes. American Marines had landed on Cape Gloucester; and In Burma, Chinese troops had achieved some success against the Japanese.

1944 had arrived by the time I finally dragged myself upstairs to bed. Mum still wasn't home, the rainwater was dripping into the buckets; Mr. Ball was still coughing, and I was still missing Beppo. But I had a feeling that 1944 was going to be a good year, and in a few hours' time I would be playing football with my new found friends, and I would be meeting my Granny for the first time.

The boys were waiting for me when I turned the corner, and there was a readymade place waiting for me in the team.

"We've got our Mike." Paddy shouted as soon as I appeared around the corner. I liked the sound of the 'our', it made me feel a part of the gang. I managed to score again and we won the game comfortably, but I was more excited about meeting Granny Kelly.

"She just lives up here," said Paddy as he led me up Montague Hill, "Number 5 Duke Street." I didn't know what to expect, although I was expecting an inquisition. The front door was ajar when we arrived at 5 Duke Street and Paddy marched into the hallway. I stood back and hesitated, waiting behind him. "Come on," he waved me on, and I detected just a touch of annoyance in his voice. The door to Granny's front room was also open, and this time, Paddy hesitated. He knocked gently on the door and waited.

"Alright Gran?" He enquired, but there was no reply. He shrugged his shoulders, made a face, and then peeped around the door. "It's only our Mike, Gran. I've brought him down to see you." Still there was no reply and Paddy turned to face me.

"She's praying. If I was you, I'd Just go on in and wait on the sofa." He placed a reassuring hand on my shoulder. "You'll be alright," he said, "I'll see you later," and then he was gone.

I tiptoed into the room. My Granny was sitting in a rocking chair, gently swaying back and forth. She was holding a rosary in her hands, and she was praying silently as she rocked. Her eyes were closed and her gnarled old fingers were racing around the beads as she silently whispered her prayers to Jesus. I stood and studied her. My Granny wasn't a witch after all. In fact, she was very much a proper granny. She had soft, shining, snow white hair, which was swept back and styled into a bun. The bun was then secured by a large and ornate mother of pearl hair comb. She was dressed entirely in black, apart from a white lace shawl which was draped across her shoulders.

I stood still and silent, not quite sure what to do next, but I felt Granny was aware of my presence and after a minute or so, she stopped praying. She didn't open her eyes, but she pointed towards the tiny sofa.

"Sit yourself down, Michael, and I'll be with you shortly. I just have one more decade of the rosary to complete."

I sat on the sofa and studied Granny and her room. It was a tiny room and sparsely furnished. There was just the rocking chair in the centre of the room, the sofa in the bay window recess, and a small dining table. There was an odd musty smell about the place, which was almost, but not quite, masked by the smell of the two scented candles which were burning in front of a small statue of the Virgin

Mary in the far corner of the room. The walls were full of pictures of Jesus and his crucifixion, and of his sacred heart. There was just a solitary photograph of a non-religious nature. It depicted a young man wearing a multi coloured shirt, a riding cap and breeches. He was carrying a whip and was sitting astride a huge chestnut horse.

I was watching Granny's lips as she rattled through the final sequence of the decade. She prayed aloud for the finale. "Glory be to the Father, and to the Son, and to the Holy Spirit. As it was in the beginning, is now, and ever shall be, world without end. Amen. She slowly made the sign of the cross, opened her eyes and studied me.

"Come here, Michael," She said eventually and motioned me to join her. She placed her hands on my head, and then gently ran her fingers over my face She stroked my forehead, my cheeks, my nose and finally my lips and mouth. I could see tears running down her cheeks.

"Oh Joe," she sobbed, "Oh Joe, Joe; to think I ever doubted he was yours." She took a handkerchief from her sleeve, wiped her eyes and blew her nose. "I suppose you are hungry."

I nodded, but she was already out of her chair and heading for the kitchen. I noticed her swollen legs and I wondered how she had managed to pour them into the tiny pair of slippers she was wearing. I stood up, crossed the room and studied the photo of the young man and his horse. The man looked very much like my father. There was some writing on the bottom of the photo. It read 'Jonjo O'Kelly, The Curragh, 1875'. I made a note to look up The Curragh in my dictionary when I got home.

"That's your Grandfather," I jumped, I hadn't heard Granny return, "that photo was taken at the Curragh, just before he came over to England. The Curragh is the most famous race course in Ireland." She handed me a plate containing four sausage sandwiches and a large slice of fruit cake. I knew right there and then that I was going to love Granny Kelly.

The sausage sandwiches were good, but I wasn't able to relax. Mum had warned me to expect an inquisition, and I knew I needed to concentrate. I ate in silence and allowed Granny to do the talking. "He was a good man, your Grandfather," she smiled, "unless he had the drink in him." She shook her head sadly. "It's the curse of the male Kelly line. Drink, and that little bit of skin between their legs has been the downfall of each and every one of them. I hope you don't go the same way, Michael."

I grunted in reply. I had learnt a long time ago, that when the female inquisition started, a grunt was the safest means of communication. It had to be a very special grunt, one that sounded nothing like either a 'yes' or a 'no'. In the face of constant vague grunting I'd found that the inquisition usually faded away.

I'm not really sure whether Granny was questioning me or not that day back in 1944. She spoke in strange, incomplete sentences and I couldn't work out exactly what she was after. I happily let her chat away whilst I carried on chewing and grunting, and then it was time to go. She gave me a long, very slobbery kiss, and I could feel her whiskers rubbing against my face, but I didn't mind, because she pressed a three penny piece into my palm as she kissed me goodbye, and everything felt good.

"Make sure you come again, and don't leave it too long."

With my belly full of sausage sandwiches and cake, and with the coin burning a hole in my pocket, there was little doubt that I would return. Anyway, apart from the food and the money, she was also my Granny, and I loved her.

8 GROWING UP FAST

Looking back across the years, I think that 1944 probably brought me greater happiness than any other period of my life. Not only had I discovered the joys of close friendship and the love of even more family members, but I was also enjoying every single moment of my time at school. My beloved teacher, Miss Lynch, had brought her very own special brand of magic to my school chores. Every day she brought me another adventure; a new book or another new word. I had, quite simply, not only fallen in love with reading and writing, but I also enjoyed the fulsome praise that Miss Lynch constantly lavished on me for my efforts. I loved all that praise, even though it usually resulted in Leonard Mills kicking me under the desk, and calling me 'teacher's fucking pet'.

Mr. Barnidge, or 'Jasper' as he was called by the boys, was the Headmaster of St Mary on the Quay, Roman Catholic Boy's School. He was a big man in every sense of the word. He was tall and powerfully built, with a low, gruff voice, a big purple nose, huge feet and massive hands. Grasped in those massive hands, he always held the ultimate symbol of his power; his thick brown cane. As far as I could tell, Mr. Barnidge didn't teach any particular subject. He just cruised silently around the school. He moved quietly through the playground, the corridors and the classrooms, imposing law, order and discipline as he went. He could silence a group of rowdy pupils with just a single withering glance from fifty paces away, and for the naughtier pupils there was always the cane. Canings were frequent and always very public. They were almost a ritual, a ceremony, and I had already witnessed many in the short time I had attended the school.

I was about to witness another caning on that Monday morning in early February 1944, but this time it was slightly different. This time it was my hand that the cane was about to descend on, and my face on which the pain would be etched. My crime had been not only skipping Holy Mass on the Sunday morning, but I had compounded matters by trying to lie my way out of it when confronted by Mr. Barnidge. It wasn't the first time I'd skipped Mass, but up until now I had been able to avoid detection. My early religious fervour was starting to cool, as I had reluctantly accepted that my ambition to become a Saint was not going to be fulfilled. I told too many lies, and hard though I tried, I knew I couldn't stop.

As I stood in front of Mr. Barnidge with my hand extended, my thoughts turned to Wilf Copping, the famous 'hard man' of pre-war English football. I'd read a lot about Mr. Copping and his famous sayings. Copping was known as a hard and strong player; his most famous quote was "the first man in a tackle never gets hurt". He also said "Never let them see that it hurts." I pictured Mr. Copping's face and braced myself. I was ready to face the cane.

"Don't muff it Sonny", growled 'Jasper'. This was his standard prelude to the beating. "Don't muff it," he repeated, and down came the cane. Just before it landed, I saw Miss Lynch wince and turn away, and then I saw Leonard Mills grinning like a Cheshire Cat. I didn't let Leonard see how much that blow had hurt me, but I never missed Mass again during the remainder of my time at the school. I did, however, continue to tell a few little lies.

The Eugene Street gang sat wide eyed and attentive, listening to every word, as I told my story about the caning. I did exaggerate it slightly, and they were very impressed. I felt that my story about the punishment had elevated me to almost celebrity status within the gang. The boys had all welcomed me in with open arms anyway, and I was already on first name terms with all of them, but I could now clearly see respect in their eyes. We played football in the street whenever it was possible, and the standard was getting higher by the week. There were more and more people watching us play now. They hung from the windows of the blocks of flats and shouted encouragement and criticism. Two men from the Bristol Royal Infirmary Boiler Room joined the spectators. They stood directly behind the goalmouth, dressed in their oily white overalls. They drank tea from chipped enamel mugs and smoked their cigarettes as they watched. They did a lot of loud shouting, and as they sounded as if they knew what they were talking about, we took notice of them. Very soon the air was full of high pitched young voices screaming 'Man on', 'Get bloody rid of it', and 'Keeper's ball.'

I knew that I was getting stronger and faster, because I had cut my personal best time for the run from home to Mr. Smith's Fish and Chip shop, from 24 to 21. It was a big improvement and I just wished that Sydney Wooderson had known about it. He would have been proud of me.

Although we had nothing we had everything; because we had each other and this was perfectly illustrated on Saturdays. Saturday was our favourite day of the week. We met up early and headed off to the News Theatre for the weekly 'Tuppenny Rush'. We were like four little old men as we trudged off in our hobnailed boots and torn and tattered short trousers. It was always the same route; down Whitson Street, across the Haymarket and up past the bomb damaged shops in Union Street. The News Theatre stood almost in solitary splendour, alongside the ruins of St Peter's Church. We stood in the queue and chatted away about football, the war, school and food, or rather the lack of it. We each had a handful of pennies clinking in our pockets and we felt like little millionaires. We were always early, and always grabbed the best seats. For an hour or so we forgot our troubles and lost ourselves in that magic silver screen. We stamped our feet in time with the rousing music as we clapped and cheered the Cowboys to their inevitable victory over the Indians. I never let on to anyone, but in truth, I was secretly cheering for the Indians. We cheered as the Newsreel showed British victories in battles on land, at sea and in the air, and we roared with laughter at the antics of the Three Stooges.

When it was over, we would pool what remained of our pennies and we headed off for home. Usually, the conversation centred on the Three Stooges. We all disliked Moe who was the dominant one, the leader, and we all felt sorry for Larry and Curly who were the constant butt of Moe's bullying. We always spent what remained of our money on either an ice cream from Mrs. Ricci's shop at the bottom of Montague Street, or on a bag of chips from Joe Stafford's Fish and Chip shop, which was further up on the corner of Dighton

Street. After that it was non-stop football until darkness, hunger or fatigue, or sometimes all three set in. They were good days; happy, carefree days.

Mum wanted to know the ins and outs of everything when I arrived home from my first visit to Granny Kelly's house. I gave her a word by word account of our conversation and she appeared to be satisfied. She roared with laughter when I told her I couldn't understand what Granny had been talking about.

"She talks in proverbs and sayings," she explained "and always only says the half of it." She took a piece of paper and started scribbling. "Here," she smiled, "Study this."

Mum had written down a list of proverbs and sayings, together with explanations. I studied the page until I was word perfect. I was now ready for another visit to Granny Kelly, and ready for another inquisition.

Granny rocked slowly in her chair and studied me closely. "What have you been up to?" she enquired eventually.

"Playing football and reading." There was nothing sinister in that question, and I sat back and relaxed.

"Like father," said Granny.

'Like son,' said the voice in my head. I liked that sentiment, and felt a wave of pride sweep over me.

Granny padded out to the kitchen, and I waited patiently for the food to arrive. She didn't disappoint. "The way to a man's heart," she said as she placed the plate of sandwiches and the slice of cake on my lap. 'Is through his stomach,' said the voice inside my head, and I found myself nodding approvingly. Granny was good; she knew what she was talking about.

Granny fell silent as I munched my way happily through the sausage sandwiches and the cake, but I didn't relax. Through the silence, I could almost hear her brain ticking over. I knew that an inquisition was just around the corner, and I didn't have to wait long.

"How's that Madge?" The alarm bells started to ring; now I knew I needed to concentrate.

"Mum's fine," I paused, "she's very busy; working hard."

"I bet she is," Granny almost whispered the words under her breath, but I heard them.

"Whilst the cat's away," she added in her normal voice.

'The mice will play,' said the voice inside my head.

"Is she still seeing that Maggie Reilly?" Granny was warming to her task now. Again, I wondered how Granny contrived to know so much without carrying out any observations. I decided she must have an informant. Inspector Goddard had an informant. Nick the Greek gave him lots of information and all for the price of just a couple of pints in the Green Man.

There was no point in trying to lie about Mrs. Reilly, because Granny clearly knew the truth.

"Yes, she still sees her," I replied.

"Birds of a feather," said Granny.

'Flock together,' said the voice inside my head and I remained silent, because that fact couldn't be denied.

"Have you heard from your father?" said Granny.

"Not for six months and several days," I replied in an instant. I was able to be that precise because I'd overheard Mum giving Mrs. Reilly this very piece of information only the previous week

"Well, I hope he's having a good time," said Granny. "What's good for the goose,"

'Is good for the gander,' said the voice inside my head. I wanted the inquisition to finish now, and I rose to my feet.

"Mum's giving up one of her jobs in order to spend more time with us," Mum had requested that I gave Granny this bit of information.

Granny sniffed derisively. "Fine words," The voice in my head remained silent and I felt a vague sense of annoyance. Granny always seemed to end our conversations with a saying I didn't know. I tried, but failed not to make a face as Granny gave me that whiskery, slobbery goodbye kiss, but I took the three penny piece and placed it in my coat pocket.

The night was growing cold as I made my way home along Eugene Street, and I was grateful for my navy blue raincoat. It was still far too big for me, and Madame Bessell had clearly lied when she said I would grow into it, but it did keep me warm and dry.

Lieutenant Fairbairn had been wearing his blue raincoat in the chapter of the book which I had read earlier that evening. He had dined out on Caviar, Lobster and Champagne. I had looked up all three in my dictionary, and didn't like the sound of any of them. I had actually felt sorry for Fairbairn that he had never sampled the joys of Granny Kelly's sausage sandwiches, but just as Lieutenant Fairbairn had done, I patted my stomach and murmured "A repast fit for a King," and just as Fairbairn had also done, I turned up the collar of my raincoat to a jaunty angle, tied a casual knot in my belt, and sauntered slowly into the night.

I stepped back into the shadows and the darkness as the doors of the King David Hotel swung open. The tall red headed man who always left on the dot of nine o'clock stood, wedged in the entrance with his arms outstretched, holding both doors open. There were the usual good natured shouts from inside, requesting that he closed the doors, but I knew that he would remain in that position for a full three or four minutes. The majority of the regulars at the King David Hotel were creatures of habit, and the man with red hair was no exception. He stood in the open doorway, puffing out his cheeks and blowing, as he adjusted to the outside temperature and prepared himself for another unsteady journey home. The evening had turned cold and I could clearly see his breath as it hit the night air.

The King David Hotel was on the corner at the bottom of St Michael's Hill. It formed the junction with Upper Maudlin Street and Perry Road, and it was the perfect spot for me to carry out my observations. I was becoming good at the observations; Inspector Goddard had taught me well, and he would have been proud of me. I took a few paces into the road, and craned my neck, so as to give myself a clear view into the bar.

"Ay oop lad," I whispered. All the regulars were in there.

The two men who looked like brothers were sitting at their usual table in the far corner. They were so much alike they could even have been twins. They had similar prominent bone structures, and they had identical bulbous noses and thick rubbery lips. Each of them also had the same little patch of greasy, black curly hair, which sat like a tiny island in the middle of a sea of baldness.

As was always the case, the younger, taller man was doing all the talking. I could see his rubbery lips going nineteen to the dozen as he spat out his monologue. He was like the conductor of an orchestra. His voice was his music, and his long bony index finger was his baton as it stabbed the air, accentuating every syllable of every word he uttered.

The older brother appeared to have long since given up any hope of joining in the conversation. He just sat there quietly, nodding in agreement. He paused, from time to time, to drink some of his beer, before returning to his nodding, and he always nodded in unison with the jabbing finger.

On an adjoining table sat the man I called 'Lord Haw-Haw'. I was convinced he was a German spy. He was a tall, thin, older man, with swept back silver hair, and he wore a pair of rimless spectacles which perched on the very end of his pointed nose. He was always immaculately dressed, and tonight was no exception. He was wearing a dark blue, three piece suit, with a white shirt, and a dark blue tie, which was secured with a gold tie pin. His dark overcoat was neatly folded and placed on a chair by his side. He was sipping an amber coloured liquid from a small glass, and after each sip he would pull a face, before taking a long swig from his pint of beer.

'Lord Haw-Haw' was another creature of habit and, as was his custom, he was reading the Daily Express. At least, he was purporting to read the Daily Express. I could see quite clearly that he was, in fact, peering around the edge of the newspaper. The true object of his attention was the woman seated on the high stool at the far end of the bar. She was wearing a white dress with a striking red and green floral pattern, and a matching pair of green strapped high heeled shoes. She was seated cross legged, right over left, and the bottom of her dress had ridden up exposing an almost indecent amount of stockinged thigh. She appeared to be lost in her own thoughts as she sat, staring into space and holding a small glass containing something red in her left hand, and a cigarette in the other. She was idly tapping the cigarette into a large glass ash tray, which was on the bar. The green strapped high heeled shoe on her right foot was hanging loose, and it was flapping rather precariously as she tapped her foot in perfect time with the tapping cigarette. I decided that she had a song going on inside her head.

Her companion was a shorter woman with a shock of shiny, black curly hair. She was wearing a bottle green, two piece suit and a white shirt. The suit was probably a size too small for her and this had the unfortunate effect of converting a few of her curves into rather unflattering tiny rolls of fat. Despite this she was extremely beautiful, and had a loud infectious laugh. She leant across and whispered something into the seated woman's ear. They both burst out laughing, but the joke must have caught the other woman either mid puff of her cigarette, or mid swig of her drink, because she began to cough, splutter and choke. She waved her hands helplessly in the air, and her friend quickly took the glass from her hand. A tall American soldier appeared from nowhere, and with a slow shake of his head and a smile, he took the cigarette from her other hand and stubbed it out in the ash tray. He was wearing a leather jacket with three stripes on his sleeve. He then produced an immaculate white handkerchief and tidied up the debris from the spluttering, the coughing and the snorting. He dabbed gently around her mouth, then across her lap and finally around her cleavage. For one moment I thought 'Lord Haw-Haw' was going to explode, and then the doors closed, and the red haired man began his unsteady journey up St Michael's Hill.

I shivered involuntarily and realised I had grown cold, hungry and tired; it had been a long day. I had contemplated wearing my raincoat, but one further challenge lay ahead of me, and that coat would have been an impediment. I looked around self-consciously and then adopted the classic middle distance athlete's starting position. I leant forward slightly with my left leg slightly bent and stretched in front of me; my right leg was also bent, but trailed behind. My arms were ready to start pumping. I was now Sydney Wooderson; I had a new record in my sights.

'On your marks: get set: go.' I heard the sound of the starting pistol in my head, and I set off at a very steady pace. I knew from painful experience that a steady pace was essential if I were to stand any chance of success. I'd made this run between the King David Hotel and my home in Halsbury Road on dozens of occasions, and my record of 453 had proven stubbornly difficult to beat. I'd been trying for a period of over three months.

28-29-30. I trotted past the King David and then past Mr. Gotsell's Butcher's shop, with its striking, vivid blue tiled shop front. The Eglington Arm's came next. Mr. Warriner would be behind the bar, pulling the pints, and would shortly be calling 'Last orders please, Ladies and Gentlemen.'

64-65-66. Johnny Ball Lane was over to my right, and Terrell Street coming up on my left. I prayed that nobody would come staggering out of the White Hart as I passed the entrance. I could see Mr. Munday in his fish and chip shop on the opposite corner. He was still wearing his white jacket and hat as he cleaned his gleaming silver frying range. He was wringing out his damp cloth in his bowl of warm water. I'd been in there earlier and spent the three penny piece that Granny had given me. I'd bought a large bag of chips and some scrumps.

96-97-98, my hobnailed boots clattered against the cobblestones, creating a steady, rhythmic, almost hypnotic beat like that of a galloping horse. The freshly painted yellow sign above the entrance to Mrs. Latus's tobacconist shop was creaking and groaning as it swung gently in the soft evening breeze. The sign read 'Capstan Full Strength', and Paddy had said that Capstan Full Strength cigarettes could 'blow your head off', and 'only real men and sailors smoked them'.

134-135-136. The Headquarters' of the Church Lad's Brigade and the Prince Alfred pub on the corner of Lower Maudlin Street were now in view, and Alfred Hill Steps appeared on my left. The gentle downhill slope of Upper Maudlin Street gave way to the gentle uphill slope of Marlborough Street.

176-177-178. I now had the Bristol Royal Infirmary on either side of me, and I was still going strong.

199-200-201. I passed Mr. Keeler's pawn shop and I was almost exactly on schedule. 'Wooderson swings into the straight.' The 'straight', was in fact the imposing 1:4 gradient of Marlborough Hill, and momentarily I was in trouble as the slope took its toll. My chin dropped onto my chest and my whole body slumped forward, but I gritted my teeth, shortened my stride and quickened the pace. Almost immediately, I regained the rhythm.

240-241-242. I was passing Eugene Street Flats now and I noticed a light was flickering in the window of Number 2. Johnny and Frankie lived there. I wondered if they were still up and listening to the radio.

297-298-299. Alfred Place and Mrs. King's corner shop on my left and Blenheim Square to my right. The Hynam family lived at the far end of Blenheim Square. I wondered whether Valerie and Nita were safely tucked up in bed.

346-347-348, my race was almost run. I passed Cleveland Road to my left and Aggie Pascoe's house to my right. My throat was burning and my heart was thumping fit to burst. I tried to conjure up an image of Jack Lovelock, the New Zealand athlete who had been Wooderson's nemesis in pre-war athletic events. I had watched that famous race on the BritishPathe Newsreel. It was the race when my hero had stormed away from Lovelock in the home straight.

389-390-391, now was the moment; I had reached Marlborough Hill Place; it was time for the final sprint.

'Wooderson produces his world famous sprint finish.' My legs had already turned to jelly, but I threw back my head and willed myself to complete the final fifty yards. I collapsed at the finishing line, which was the red brick wall of number 12.

424. I'd not just beaten, but I'd smashed my record, and deep inside I somehow knew it would never be bettered again. I lay on the pavement in an exhausted panting heap, and as I slowly recovered, I stared out into the absolute darkness that was 'blackout Bristol'. From time to time a glimmer of light would briefly penetrate the darkness. It was probably a light from some unknown car, driven by a complete stranger in some remote street in East Bristol. The light would always disappear very quickly.

'Put that bloody light out.' Said the voice inside my head. That was the cry that used to echo around our streets, when Bristol had been a city was under siege. It was the warning call from the brave ARP wardens who were out there on patrol. I smiled to myself as I recalled how Mum would leap to her feet whenever we heard that shout. How she would race across the room, and tug away nervously at the curtains; just in case ours was the offending window. The blitz was all a distant memory now, but it was a memory that hadn't faded. We all still lived in fear. Fear of once again waking in the night to the sound of the wailing air raid sirens and the throbbing drone of the German planes flying overhead. We were all still very conscious of the black-out.

Our house was in complete darkness as I wandered up the garden path and took the front door key from its home beneath the brick on the coalhouse floor. I opened the front door, replaced the key beneath the brick and slid the bolt home. It was important that I always remembered to slide the bolt. The last, and only time I'd forgotten had been the night before Beppo had disappeared and died. I still felt guilty about that, and knew that I always would.

I removed my boots, threw some coals on the smouldering embers of the fire, lit a candle and climbed the stairs to my bedroom. There were thirty nine stairs from bottom to top, and twenty nine of them contained squeaky floor boards. This wasn't a problem; I knew the position of each of those floor boards, and I could complete a squeak free climb with my eyes closed. I stopped off on the first floor to say goodnight to Mary. She was fast asleep; her dark curls spread out over the white pillow. Her thumb was in her mouth, and she was sucking contentedly as she dreamed her dreams. I kissed the tips of my fingers and placed them on her cheek, just as Jacob had done to Mum all those years earlier. She stirred, but she didn't wake and I crept quietly away.

The landing outside of Mum's bedroom was a minefield of squeaking floorboards, but I quickly and easily found my way through them and reached my own room without mishap. I removed the buff coloured exercise book and pencil from their hiding place, beneath my mattress, and by the light of the flickering candle, I made up the notes of my observations. I was very pleased with the night's work and I snuggled up to my hot water bottle; I was ready for sleep and some pleasant dreams.

I was just dozing off when I heard the voices. I went to the window and looked down. They were just turning the corner. Mum had given up completely on the green strapped high heeled shoes. She was carrying both of them now in her left hand. She was wearing the leather jacket with the three stripes on the arm. Buddy was walking immediately behind her, lovingly holding her elbows in the palms of his hands; gently guiding her as she tiptoed nervously across the cobblestones in her stockinged feet. Mrs. Reilly was walking behind, arm in arm with Lucas. She was still chattering and giggling. Mum turned to her, raised a cautionary finger to her lips and pointed up in the direction of my room. I heard the key turn in the door and then I heard clunk of coins as they fell into the empty electricity meter. I heard Buddy's voice and then they all laughed. I placed the pillow over my head and tried to sleep. Just before I dropped off, I wondered to myself what Dad would say when he came home from the war, and I showed him my observations.

9 ALL THE GIRLS IN FRANCE

There were about a dozen of us taking shelter from the sudden, early morning storm. The unexpected downpour had taken us completely by surprise and had interrupted the precious pre-school football match in the playground. We lounged around, leaning against the ornate stone pillars, which supported the corrugated iron roof of the open fronted shed, and prayed for the blue skies to return before Mr. Stirrup appeared to ring the big brass bell which would summon us in for lessons. It wasn't to be, and as the time slipped away, the rain continued to drum down on the old tin roof, and Leonard Mills held court with a growing and attentive audience.

All the girls in France
Do the belly wobble dance,
Singing Nelly put your belly close to mine.
All the girls in Spain
Wash their knickers in the rain,
Singing Nelly put your belly close to mine.

Leonard could certainly sing in tune, and it was a catchy little melody, but it was the lyrics which fired our imaginations and caused us all to roar with laughter. Suitably encouraged by the reaction, Leonard sang it again, but this time he substituted 'Kelly' for 'Nelly' and this made it even funnier. The laughter was louder and longer. In fact, it was sufficiently loud to briefly bring Mr. Stirrup's head out into the rain as he poked it around the door, his experienced eyes suspiciously scanning the yard, looking for any signs of trouble.

There was no stopping Leonard now, and he was in full flow as he proceeded to describe, in graphic detail, exactly what happened when a man and woman performed the 'belly wobble dance' together and made a baby. Some of the boys looked shocked, but I'd heard it all before; Mum had told me about it some years earlier, and we boys chatted about it for hours after our football matches in Eugene Street had ended.

Leonard still hadn't finished. He now produced a piece of paper from his pocket on which he had drawn a cartoon. He told us it depicted Miss Lynch doing the 'belly wobble dance' with me. Underneath the drawing he had written in large capital letters, KELLY THE TEECHERS PET.

The boys were still roaring with laughter when Mr. Stirrup appeared again, this time to ring the big brass bell which summoned us to lessons. I wasn't laughing though, and neither was Miss Lynch when she discovered the drawing in Leonard's exercise book later that day. Mr. Barnidge wasn't laughing either as he bellowed "Don't muff it sonny," and then he brought the cane crashing down twice on Leonard's outstretched hand. I decided the extra stroke must have been for the poor spelling. I tried not to grin like a Cheshire cat, but I probably failed, because as he returned to his seat, Leonard kicked me hard on my shins, underneath the desk.

"Life is like a book," said Mum as she prepared me for school. "There are happy pages and there are sad pages, and some pages which do nothing for you at all, but if you wish to learn, and you keep your eyes open, there is a new lesson to be learnt every day."

I had a sentence from a book buzzing around in my head. It was a simple little sentence; just a collection of words about the Arctic which I had read in a magazine I had found on Mum's bed. For some unknown reason, that sentence had captured my imagination and I'd memorised it; word by word, and punctuation mark by punctuation mark. I was determined to use it, if and when the opportunity ever arose, and the opportunity came sooner than I'd expected.

"Dreams that we remember are very precious moments," Miss Lynch rose from her desk and walked slowly up and down in front of us, her hands clasped as if in prayer. "I want you all to think hard and try to recall one such dream, and write me a composition about it."

I could barely contain my excitement as I relived that article from Mum's magazine. I wrote about snowflakes and glaciers; about Polar Bears and Caribou; about Ice Bergs and frozen lakes; about Arctic Foxes and Wolves; about Seals and a Walrus. I finished my composition with that sentence. 'A silver falcon hovered by, swooped, picked up a lemming and flew off.' Then my dream and my composition ended. It was my best ever work of fiction, and I was very proud of it.

Miss Lynch was also impressed, but there was a slight problem. Leonard Mills, who was seated next to me, had included that very same sentence in his composition.

"Leonard," Miss Lynch enquired. "What pray tell me is a Lemming?" Leonard didn't have a clue, and I actually felt a wave of compassion as Mr. Barnidge growled his 'Don't muff it Sonny' speech before bringing the cane down again on Leonard's outstretched hand. Predictably, Leonard kicked me under the desk as he returned to his seat.

Miss Lynch wrote 'excellent', in red ink at the bottom of the page and told me to take the composition home to show Mum. I was meeting Mum and Mary outside of the Colston Hall that afternoon, as Mary had an appointment at Tower Hill Clinic. It was raining heavily, and I took shelter on the steps of the Colston Hall and watched the old man as he worked in the rain. He was sweeping the pavements outside of the Theatre, and then, as the rain stopped, he came onto the steps for a cigarette and I ventured out to admire the highly polished black motor car parked directly in front of me. I studied the raindrops which had collected on the gleaming surface, and then gently ran my index finger along the bonnet. I was amazed at the way the droplets flew off, and then immediately reformed in perfect symmetry.

"What are you doing to my car?" The hand on my left shoulder held me in a vice like grip.

"Nothing," I replied rather lamely.

The owner of the car was middle aged, short, portly, and had a black moustache. He was wearing a dark suit, a dark blue overcoat and black bowler hat.

"Don't touch what doesn't belong to you," he hissed through gritted teeth, and then he spotted the composition in my hand.

"What have you got there?" He snatched the two pieces of paper from my grasp, gave them a cursory glance, and then tore them into small pieces before dropping them into a puddle. "Keep away from my car."

I watched him drive off, and I kicked at the ground in anger.

"Bloody Councillors and Freemasons," said the old man with the broom. "They think they know everything and own the bloody place. They think everything's about them." He lit another cigarette and returned to his sweeping. "Don't grow up to be one of them son."

I didn't tell Mum about the incident, but I knew I'd learnt another lesson in life.

I was approaching my seventh birthday now and it would shortly be time for me to make my first confession. I had, up until now, been reasonably relaxed about it. I had carefully studied and learnt the Ten Commandments. I had examined my conscience as instructed by Father Doyle, and I'd decided that apart from the many lies I had told, I was free from sin and in a comparative state of grace. Father Doyle had then given me a checklist which had rapidly shattered all my illusions. It was a list of potential venial sins, and I didn't have to look very closely at that list to realise that far from being free from sin, I was a multiple serial sinner.

The following were all sins, and I was guilty on all counts.

Did I pay attention at Mass?

Have I fooled around in Church?

Did I say my prayers every day?

Did I say mean things to my Mum or Dad?

Did I always say "Thank You" to people?

Am I hard to get along with (during school, at Grandma's, at home?)?

Did I do what my Mum or Dad or Teacher told me to do?

Was I lazy around the house?

Did I do my chores?

Did I hurt others people's feelings by calling them bad names?

Have I started fights with my brothers and sisters at home?

Have I blamed other people for things I do?

Did I get other people into trouble?

Do I hit people when I get mad?

Have I forgiven people? Or am I holding a grudge?

Have I cheated or been unfair in games?

Did I refuse to play with someone for no good reason?

Was I was lazy about my schoolwork?

Did I fail to do my homework?

Did I cheat in school?

How many times did I lie to my parents, my teachers, or my friends?

Did I take anything that didn't belong to me?

Did I avoid medicine? Did I refuse to eat food I didn't like?

I counted twenty three sins which I now needed to confess. As I agonised over that list, Father Doyle was telling Mum another of his stories. It was about the Good Samaritan. I had one eye on my checklist and one ear on the story; it was yet another good one. Father Doyle explained to Mum how the two people who had walked past the injured man without assisting him were equally as guilty as the robbers.

"They were also sinners. They had committed sins of omission," he said by way of explanation.

I was beginning to realise just how hard it was to be a good Catholic and to get into heaven. Not only were all the things I did classed as 'sins', but now it appeared that many of the things I didn't do were 'sins'. In fact, I had come to the conclusion that heaven was only for the likes of Granny Kelly and people like her, who just sat in their rocking chairs, saying prayers all day, and handing out sausage sandwiches, three penny pieces and kisses; or like Rosie Tedesco who sang very loudly at the back of the church and never ever had to look at the hymn book for help with the words; or people like the two Capel sisters who went to Mass every day of every week of the year. The Capel sisters lived in Marlborough Hill Place and they walked down the hill every morning at the same time. They were blessed with both beauty and grace and I used to loiter outside of Mrs. Latus's shop knowing they would be buying their morning newspaper on the way to church. If I ever managed to time it right, I was sometimes rewarded with a smile or a nod of acknowledgement from one or both of them. When I was, it felt as if I had been touched by an angel, and the feeling lasted me all day.

My daydreams were interrupted by Father Doyle shouting as he addressed Mum.

"Sex," he roared "is an act of love between a husband and a wife; performed within the confines of Holy Matrimony and in the marital bed." The little vein in his forehead was throbbing again. "Anything else is a gross violation of the Ten Commandments, and a grievous mortal sin against Holy Purity, be it by thought, word or deed. The offenders will burn and rot in the flames of hell."

Mum was staring vacantly into space as she chewed away at the inside of the right hand corner of her lips. This was a face she usually reserved for when she was working out the household budget, and was a sure sign that she was very worried. In truth, we were both worried. In addition to the twenty three venial sins, I had just realised that the 'belly wobble dance' was about 'sex', and I also had one of those 'grievous mortal sins' to confess. I began to look for a way out of it.

"Dirty old bugger," said Mum as the door closed behind Father Doyle. "Why are the Catholics so obsessed with sex?"

May has always been my favourite month of the year, and not just because it contains my birthday. It's a month that has this habit of throwing up the most unexpectedly delightful day. Friday, May 19th 1944, was one such day. It was also my birthday, I was 7, and I was another day closer to being grown up. Mum had already made it quite clear there were to be no presents, greeting cards or parties, but she'd promised to buy me the 'biggest pig's trotter in Bristol' for my tea that night.

As I stood at the open window of my bedroom that morning, there was just the merest hint of winter remaining in the air, but the sky was blue and the sun, which was just rising over the hills of Purdown, to the east, was full of promise for later in the day.

I quite often disliked Fridays. Mum always did her housekeeping budget on a Thursday night. She sat at the table for hour after hour, chewing on the end of her pencil as she shuffled and shifted her coins around from one pile to another, and worked and then reworked her arithmetic until she had balanced the books. I always watched her closely, hoping and praying that there would be sufficient money left over to pay the rent.

Mum had warned me when she'd appointed me as 'man of the house', that there would be times when I would have to 'sing for my supper', and dealing with Mr. Meredith, the rent collector, was just one of the many songs I had to sing. Mum didn't like Mr. Meredith and neither did I.

He always called early on Friday morning and knocked on the door with a very distinctive triple rat-a-tat-tat. He was an odd little man, who always wore a heavy tweed overcoat and fingerless blue woollen gloves, whatever the weather. We never spoke, but greeted each other with a nod. I would hand him the money and the rent book, and then I would stand and study the permanent dew drop on the end of his nose whilst he entered the payment in the rent book. He wrote in that same immaculate copper plate handwriting that Miss Lynch used. Once the ink had dried, he wiped away the dew drop with the back of his glove, handed me back the book, nodded again and then left.

Whenever we didn't have the money, we just hid under the table whilst Mr. Meredith circled the bay windows seeking out gaps in the curtain, tapping on the glass and calling Mum's name. I didn't like it under the table, and I didn't like it either when I had to break cover and wander outside to check that he wasn't still lurking around.

That morning was one of the good days when the money was available. It was a splendid start to my birthday and I knew it was destined to be a special day. It got even better when I timed my arrival outside of Mrs. Latus's shop to perfection and had both a smile and a nod from each of the Capel sisters. I almost fainted with pleasure when the taller one said "Good morning Michael."

The rest of the day was largely uneventful. I scored a couple of goals in the playground; Miss Lynch wrote 'excellent' in red ink on my composition and then read it out to the class, and Leonard Mills kicked me underneath the desk. After school I had a couple of hours to spare before Mum and Mary were due home and I joined the boys for an after school game of football on the piece of waste ground behind The Leopard Pub, which was directly opposite Pipe Lane. That piece of ground is now the site of the first floor of the multi storey car park, but back then, was an excellent little cinder covered pitch. I had just read about Wilf Copping's famous two footed tackle that had changed the course of the England v Italy International at Highbury in 1934. A tackle which had shattered the foot of the Italian captain and resulted in England winning what my book had described as an 'ill-tempered encounter'. I had been practicing that tackle and now was the moment to try it out. Leonard Mills was my chosen target and although I didn't shatter his foot, he limped off in some discomfort.

I still had time to kill after the game, and I wandered down to The Haymarket. I loved the atmosphere there, and I enjoyed watching and listening to the newspaper man.

I heard his loud, low pitched growl long before I turned the final corner and got there.

"Een-po-she Lash-dishun," he growled. When I'd first heard that growl I had been confused and couldn't work out what he was saying, but Mum knew immediately and explained it was 'Evening Post-Last edition'.

The Haymarket was always extremely busy at that time of night. All the men were returning home from their places of work and many of them stopped to buy a newspaper. Several of them also regularly lingered to read the headlines and discuss the latest news.

"Een-po-she Lash-dishun," growled the newspaper man again. He was in his usual spot, sitting on his tiny wooden trolley with his back to the ornate metal railings of the underground ladies toilets. He lived on that trolley because he had no legs from just below his knees. He sat there wearing his usual shiny dark blue pin striped suit with the legs of his trousers folded up and over the stumps, and then secured with two extra-large safety pins. There was a little wheel on each corner of the trolley, and he propelled the trolley around the streets with the aid of two short, but sturdy pieces of metal. His forearms were like a pair of oak trees. He sat on the trolley, a large pile of newspapers on his right hand side and a leather pouch, in which he kept his takings, draped across his shoulders.

A few of the regulars were gathering now, and I moved closer trying to get within earshot. I watched them closely as they studied the headlines. The tall man with the white, nicotine stained moustache and the big black bike spoke first.

"Blige! We've taken Monte Cassino at last. It should be all over by Christmas,"

"I very much doubt it," replied the man in the dark overcoat who was carrying a brief case and a rolled up umbrella. He was very well spoken and sounded just like Alvar Lidell. I had already decided that he must be either a Councillor or a Freemason.

"But the road to Rome is wide open now." The man on the bike was insistent. 'Jerry' won't like it up 'em and it will be run rabbit run.

."We'll have to wait and see," said the man in the dark coat, "Nothing is ever that straight forward in war. "

Both men then started their regular evening ritual. They both carefully folded their newspapers and put them away. The man with the white moustache placed his in his saddle bag, and the other man placed his into his brief case. Without any further words they set off to complete the final leg of their journeys home. The man on the bike pedalled silently in the direction of Stokes Croft, and the Freemason marched off smartly towards Lower Union Street.

"Een-po-she Lash-dishun," growled the man with no legs, and the last few copies were quickly snapped up. The final few copper coins dropped into his bag with a satisfying clunk. The newspaper man prepared for his journey home. He grasped one of the railings and hauled himself around into his driving position. This was the part that always fascinated me. He tugged at the stumps of his legs as he pulled them aboard the trolley, and beat at them with one of the pieces of metal he used for driving.

"Come on you bastards," he yelled as he successfully lifted the stumps on to his trolley, and then he was gone. His two massive arms pumping like a pair of pistons as he shot across the road, and headed off along the Horsefair towards Milk Street, which was where Mum said he lived.

So Monte Cassino had final fallen. It was all going to be over by Christmas. I wondered what it would be like having a father for Christmas, and I hoped and prayed that Mum had bought my pig's trotter. As I trudged up Marlborough Hill, I suddenly felt blessed; I was the luckiest boy in Bristol.

The pig's trotter was, without doubt, the biggest I had ever seen, and it was by far the tastiest I had ever eaten. I tackled it with my fingers and by the time I'd finished it, both my hands and my face were plastered in grease. Mum sat with her elbows on the table and her face in her hands as she watched me chew every morsel of meat and fat from the trotter. She just sat smiling and nodding with a stupid look on her face. When I'd finished a large pile of bones sat on my empty plate. Mum reached across and tousled my hair.

"Happy birthday Michael...I love you."

I wanted badly to run around the table, to hold her and kiss her, to tell her that I loved her too, but I never did.

Mum didn't go out that night. We all sat around the fire and played games. Mum told us all the usual stories about Long Ashton and about my brothers Dennis and Ivan. At nine o'clock we sat back and listened to the news.

"Polish troops today broke through at Monte Cassino," Alvar's velvet voice whispered from the radio. "The road to Rome is now open."

"Oh my God," Mum's face was a picture.

"It will be all over by Christmas, and Dad will be home." I smiled at Mum. "Run rabbit, run rabbit, run, run, run."

"You are a funny child," said Mum.

I went to bed that night and dreamt of pig's trotters and playing football in the snow with my father at Christmas.

I slept very well; there was no rainwater dripping from the ceiling; Mr. Ball was no longer coughing, and Mr. and Mrs. Muldowney were silent again. Mum told me that Mr. Ball was in hospital and getting better, but I knew she was telling lies. I'd seen Mrs. Ball crying as she spoke with Mum across the garden fence, and I'd seen the men carrying the big brown box out of the house. I was very worried that Mr. Ball might not get into heaven because he wasn't a Catholic.

Mum wrote a note to Father Doyle explaining that she had sickness and a headache and would be unable to go to confession. She put it into a brown envelope and told me to hand it to Father Doyle.

I arrived at the church in good time and handed Mum's note to Father Doyle. He opened it, read it and grunted. He didn't say anything, but I sensed he was disappointed. I took my place in the queue for confession. I was second in line; with only Charlie Stephens ahead of me. Charlie lived on Kingsdown Parade. He was a tall, thin, silent, and intelligent boy; one of the few pupils who gave the impression of wanting to be educated. I doubted that Charlie would have much to confess. The pew outside of Father Doyle's confessional slowly filled up. By the time Charlie went in it was full. I was becoming nervous, worried that my plan wouldn't work. I noticed that Leonard Mills was at the very end of the line.

Sure enough, Charlie was in and out in a flash and I crept in quietly. Father Doyle was praying quietly but rapidly, he was speaking like a machine gun, but in Latin. He eventually fell silent and I remembered all my training. I made a sign of the cross and swallowed hard.

"Pray Father forgive me for I have sinned, this is my first confession."

The first part of my plan had been to disguise my voice, but I'd quickly abandoned this idea as my false voice sounded odd.

"And what sins have you committed my son?" The priest asked the question in that stupid tone of voice that grown-ups use when they are trying to wheedle information from a child. I was seven now, and that wouldn't work with me.

"I've told lies Father," I replied without hesitation. This was all going to plan, but the best laid plans usually go astray and my plan was no exception.

"How many lies have you told, my child?" I hadn't thought things through this far and the question came as a surprise. I had to think quickly.

"Two or three Father," I paused, and considered my options. "Or maybe four or five," I added as I realised I was in the middle of telling even more lies.

"And what other sins have you committed,"

"None Father," I replied in a voice filled with righteous indignation.

He pressed me hard, running through most of the sins in the checklist, but I stayed cool and quietly denied them all. I had decided my other sins could wait for another day. Eventually, he gave up. I could hear the annoyance in his voice when he realised he wasn't getting anywhere.

"I want you to say a good Act of Contrition and for your penance, say five Hail Marys and five Our Fathers."

It was almost all over. I closed my eyes and prayed hard.

"O my God, I am sorry and beg pardon for all my sins, and detest them above all things, because they deserve thy dreadful punishments, because they have crucified my loving Saviour, Jesus Christ, and, most of all, because they offend thine infinite goodness; and I firmly resolve, by the help of thy grace, never to offend thee again, and carefully to avoid the occasions of sin. Amen." As I prayed, Father Doyle was rattling away in Latin. We both ended our prayers at the same time.

"I absolve you from your sins in the name of the Father, the Son and the Holy Spirit, Amen."

He paused, then "Go in peace."

"Thank you father;" I was finished. As I left the confessional only Leonard Mills looked up to catch my eye. I hurried across to the central pews to say my penance and Robin Rumbelow stumbled in to take my place in the box.

I knew it was too late to catch the boys at the News Theatre now. They would be heading down Ellbroad Street, laughing and joking as they shared the bag of fish and chips and discussed the latest episode of the Three Stooges film. I felt slightly cheated, but then again, at least I was free from sin…or was I? I was sauntering along Lewin's Mead and I'd just reached Greyfriars when it dawned on me that my Confession had been a complete charade; that I had sinned badly. I was suddenly overcome with shame and remorse and I turned and headed back to church. The church seemed empty as I walked in, but just as I knelt in the central pew to say some extra prayers, Leonard Mills came limping out of the box. He looked at me in amazement, and then knelt and shuffled his way along the pew to join me.

"Are you still here? How many did you get?" Leonard tried to whisper, but his voice echoed around the empty church.

"Fifty," I replied, trying to sound tough but casual at the same time.

"What- of each?" Leonard asked, again rather loudly.

I nodded; I just wanted to say my penance and get away.

"Bloody hell, you must have been very naughty," Leonard's face was a picture of admiration. "You must have been very bad. I only got five of each and I told him about the 'belly wobble dance."

Suddenly, all my shame and remorse just melted away. I didn't stay around to say my fifty either. No sooner had Leonard hobbled off than I followed him. I suddenly had doubts about my faith, but Leonard treated me with a new respect from that day on. Mum was right; there were new lessons to be learnt every day.

10 AT THE END OF THE DAY

The world is an ever changing stage, but never more so than in wartime. In the days immediately following my birthday and my First Confession, my own little world turned upside down and everything seemed to change. Quite suddenly, most of the American troops left us. They just quietly packed their bags, their Jeeps and their Lorries and they melted away into the night. In the blink of an eye, Bristol returned to being an unrelenting sea of grey as the Bristolian males reclaimed their territory, and the streets and pavements were once more full of grey haired, grey faced, grey suited, and unsmiling men as they cycled or walked to and from their places of business. The women and the girls also changed as they suddenly lost their sparkle and their glamour. Hair nets and curlers became the fashion again and the faces in the shopping queues were once more tense, strained and worried. College Green was eerily silent at night as the wailing trumpets, saxophones and trombones no longer played the hit songs of the day. The vibrant strains of 'In the Mood' and 'Moonlight Serenade' soon became but distant memories. I never thought for a minute that I would miss those young, confident, brash handsome men who had raced around Bristol in their Jeeps, shouting at the girls and handing out the chewing gum, but I did and I missed them badly.

Then, within a few days we all sat huddled around the radio listening to John Snagge as he described the Normandy invasions.

"This is the BBC Home Service - and here is a special bulletin read by John Snagge. D-Day has come. Early this morning the Allies began the assault on the north-western face of Hitler's European fortress. The first official news came just after half-past nine, when Supreme Headquarters of the Allied Expeditionary Force issued Communique Number One. This said: 'Under the command of General Eisenhower, Allied naval forces, supported by strong air forces, and naval support began landing Allied armies this morning on the northern coast of France'.

Mrs. Reilly was at the house, drinking tea with Mum.

"Those poor boys," Mrs. Reilly said quietly. Mum sat nervously playing with her handkerchief and remained silent.

So this was it; this was the moment that we'd all been waiting for. I wondered what my friends in The Haymarket would have to say about this news. I couldn't wait to get down there and listen in to the next round of conversations.

"Een-po-she Lash-dishun" growled the Newspaper Seller. I hovered, trying to look inconspicuous. I had one eye on the man sitting on his trolley, the other on the two men absorbed in their reading. I noticed, for the first time, that the man with the white, nicotine stained moustache never actually dismounted from his bike; he always kept one foot on a pedal and the other on the ground as he tilted his bike to one side and balanced himself with an arm on the top of the ornate ironwork. He was the first to speak.

"The final push," he said quietly as he finished reading and then commenced his nightly ritual of folding and storing the newspaper.

"God bless 'em and good luck to 'em," replied the man in the blue overcoat.

They sounded more subdued than I had expected, and I felt a slight sense of disappointment as I watched them disappear into the distance. I had been anticipating a much longer conversation and far more excitement, but the disappointment didn't last long. I was at Granny Kelly's house for tea, and that meant sausage sandwiches and cake. I didn't hang around to watch the newspaper seller leave. Granny was a stickler for punctuality and being late meant going hungry. I wandered off up Whitson Street, heading towards number 5 Duke Street. I found a nice large stone and set off on a mazy dribble.

'Copping to Mathews and Mathews crosses to Drake…Goal!!!!'

Life was good and we were definitely winning the war.

Granny had news for me, and she was very excited.

"Your brother is coming up from Weymouth to see you."

I didn't reply; because I was too busy eating my sausage sandwich.

"You do know you have a brother? Your mother has told you about Dennis?"

I nodded in reply.

"She was a good woman was that Lilian."

I wanted to say that Mum was also a good woman, but I didn't. I just kept chewing.

I told Granny about the man with no legs.

"Let that be a lesson to you... I used to complain that I had no shoes, and then I met a man who had no feet." Granny smiled. "Be here about ten o'clock tomorrow please, to meet your brother."

Before I left the house the following morning, Mum warned me to be careful what I said to Dennis. I promised her I would.

I had a shock when I met my brother. I was expecting him to be a big boy. He wasn't, he was very much a young man. He was very tall, very dark and very handsome. He was wearing a plain grey flannel suit with an open necked white shirt. His hair was thick and combed back without a parting. His skin was heavily sun kissed and he would have made a very good film star or an American soldier. He not only smoked, but he smoked Capstan Full Strength, and they hadn't, as yet, 'blown his head off'.

He came forward to greet me, and then knelt down in front of me. He placed his hands on my shoulders and looked me straight in the eyes. I had blue eyes, but his were dark brown. After studying me for several minutes, he finally spoke.

"So you are my little brother," he patted my cheeks and tugged at my shoulders. "Shoulders back and stand up straight Michael; never forget you're a Kelly." He laughed; he had a wicked laugh and a cheeky smile.

Granny had already prepared our packed lunches and in addition, she gave each of us an apple.

"I'm all yours," said Dennis as we set off up Montague Hill. "Take me wherever you wish...as long as we end up at The Zoo." He laughed that wicked laugh again.

Our first port of call was Cotham Park. We sat on the grass and Dennis talked whilst I munched on my sandwiches, listening, but at the same time keeping an eye out for Peggy, but she was nowhere to be seen again. Dennis told me some stories about my father. They were all stories I had never heard before.

"The old man was handy with his mitts," Dennis adopted a boxer's pose and skipped around, puffing and blowing as he threw a series of imaginary punches. "I'm quite tidy," he continued, still throwing the punches, "but not a patch on the old man. The old man was banned from every boxing booth at every fair ground in Weymouth."

He fell silent and lit up another Capstan Full Strength cigarette. "I'm in a bit of trouble Michael. I've come up to Bristol to dispose of the evidence." He pulled several packets of cigarettes from his pocket and tapped them with the index finger of his right hand. "The evidence is being disposed of very quickly," he gave one of his wicked chuckles, "and I have established an alibi." He rubbed his chin thoughtfully. "Do you know what an alibi is?"

He was asking an expert. I had read *Goddard of the Yard* and listened to *Paul Temple*. I just prayed that Inspector Goddard wasn't on Dennis's case. He was an expert at cracking alibis. I think my big brother was impressed with my knowledge.

He was equally impressed with our next stop on the Downs. We sat in the 'Dumps', the hilly, bumpy surface in the area by Upper Belgrave Road. I ate my apple whilst Dennis smoked another two cigarettes and expressed his amazement at the wide open spaces. He sang a few lines from the song *don't fence me in*.

"You are one lucky boy living here Michael" He still hadn't touched his sandwiches. I decided he was saving them for me.

Mum had taken me to the Zoo on several occasions and I knew my way around. Dennis had plenty of money in his pockets and we had an ice cream each and shared a bottle of lemonade. We saw the monkeys and the lions; the tigers and the parrots. One of the parrots looked like Captain Flint, and I was just a little bit worried. I had a ride on Rosie the elephant. I didn't enjoy it a lot, but I kept smiling and tried not to show my fear of heights. We were having a lovely time and then it got even better. Dennis met, and fell in love with Alfred the Gorilla. It was truly love at first sight and it was mutual. They stood admiring one another. Alfred beat his chest with his hands moving like lightning and he let out some loud screaming noises. It frightened me, but Dennis stood his ground and, in turn, beat his chest and screamed back. Alfred seemed impressed.

"I love that animal," said my brother. "He's just like me. He's a perfect physical specimen and a wild, free spirit. They won't tame Alfred with bars and cages, and they won't tame Dennis Kelly either."

Alfred had every last crumb of Dennis's sandwiches and .also his apple. Dennis spoke about Alfred all the way home.

Before he left for Temple Meads, my brother knelt down in front of me and pulled my shoulders back again. "Tall, straight and proud," he said. "Remember you are a Kelly, and look after the old man when he comes home from the war. He's going to need you. Also, look after Madge. Life hasn't been kind to her either."

I watched him as he walked off down Montague Street. There were no backward glances or final waves, but he was walking tall, straight and proud. He was definitely a Kelly and he was my big brother, and I loved him.

The man with the white, nicotine stained moustache had been hopelessly wrong with his prediction. The man who was either a Councillor or a Freemason had been right to be cautious. As Christmas, 1944, drew nearer, not only was the war not over, but the German Army had launched a surprise and massive counter offensive which had inflicted record casualties to the American army. The Germans were intent on recapturing the port of Antwerp and they almost made it. The Battle of the Bulge had seen the Americans surrounded at Bastogne and it wasn't until Christmas Eve that the battle was over and we had won another vital battle.

We had rabbit stew for Christmas dinner. Money was still tight and rationing severe, but I liked rabbit stew and Mum made me an extra doughboy, because I was the 'man of the house'.

Mum and Mrs. Reilly were sat in front of the fire as I crept out on Christmas afternoon to visit Granny. They were drinking tea, and making some toast on the fire. Mrs. Reilly was sat in my armchair.

"Buddy promised to write every day and I haven't heard a word," said Mum quietly. "He's worse than Joe."

"Lucas was the same," Mrs. Reilly sipped her drink.

"Men!!" Said Mum and then cursed as she burnt her hand on the toasting fork.

"Who'd have 'em?" Mrs. Reilly took another sip..

"What would we do without 'em?" Said Mum, and then they both laughed.

We had a new teacher at school. His name was Mr. Goodway, and he was our first ever sports teacher. He was quite young and he brought with him, a proper football. A big brown leather beast that was much more difficult to control and kick than the tennis balls we had played with up until now. He took us on the bus to the Downs and taught us about the offside rule. It was very complicated but he showed me how to 'bend my run' to avoid being caught offside.

We held a trial match and he praised my two footed tackle and then announced that we would be playing a full scale game against Anglesea Place School.

"We play it hard, but we play it fair. We play it within the rules, but we play it to win." We sat on the grass, wide eyed and open mouthed, taking in every word. "Do you all understand? We are St Mary's; and we play to win!" We all nodded our agreement.

We took the bus to the Downs on the appointed day. We all sat in a nervous silence for most of the journey, but Mr. Goodway stood up from time to time and shouted "Win! Win! Win!"

Our opponents were waiting for us when we arrived. They were doing some elaborate training drills and looked far more the part than we did. They were wearing a proper football kit. It consisted of black and purple shirts, with black shorts and socks. Most of them were wearing proper football boots.

Mr. Goodway had told us to remove our shirts and we were playing in our vests, whilst wearing our normal trousers and footwear. Moggy was wearing his cut down wellington boots and I was wearing my hobnailed boots. I quickly discovered that my hobnailed boots weren't ideal for the lush grass, and it was all a bit of a struggle. On the couple of occasions when Moggy managed to release me through on goal, the Anglesea Place teacher was very quick to wave his handkerchief and shout "Offside!"

Both sides were finding it difficult and the score was still standing at 0-0 when the Referee shouted "Last minute." No sooner had he uttered the words, than Moggy managed to deliver one of his special passes. As the ball dropped behind the last defender, I bent my run and moved on to it. From the corner of my eye I saw the linesman frantically waving his handkerchief and I heard him shout 'Offside'.

"Play on," shouted the referee as he waved both arms in the air.

"Shoot," he mouthed at me as I looked up. I did just that, and sent the ball back across the goal and past the floundering young goalkeeper.

"Goal," shouted the referee, and blew his whistle. "Full time," he declared.

"He was yards offside," screamed the Anglesea Place teacher.

"Not when the ball was played. He bent his run to perfection," said the referee firmly, as he tucked the ball underneath his arm and strode off the pitch. As he passed me, he tapped his nose and smiled.

"Always play to the whistle Kelly. Be it in life or in football. If you do that, you'll win far more than you lose." The referee was Mr. Goodway, and I knew just how much he wanted to win.

Mum was right. If you paid sufficient attention, there was a lesson to be learnt from life every day.

Britain in 1945 had no supermarkets, no motorways, no teabags, no sliced bread, no flavoured crisps, no lager, no microwaves, no dishwashers, no CDs, no computers, no mobile phones, no duvets, no contraceptive pill, no trainers, no hoodies, no Starbucks. But we did have shops, pubs, and fish and chips on every corner, cinemas in every high street, red phone boxes, trams, trolley buses and steam trains. We also had Woodbines, Craven 'A' and Senior Service, smoke and smog. There were no launderettes, or automatic washing machines, but we had wash day every Monday, with the clothes boiled in a tub, then scrubbed on the draining board and rinsed in a sink, put through a mangle, then hung out to dry. We had no central heating or running hot water, but we had a coal fire, a hearth, cold sores, chilblains and Impetigo. Abortion, homo sexual relationships and suicide were all illegal. There were a handful of cars, but no such thing as seatbelts. We treated our ailments with Vick vapour rub, Vaseline, Milk of Magnesia, Fynnon salts, Andrew's Liver Salts, Enos and Germolene. Meat, butter, margarine, lard, sugar, tea, cheese, jam, eggs, sweets, soap, and clothes were all rationed. We were happy, we were winning the war. Mr. Hitler was on the run and our fathers were about to return home.

Mum had also spoken the truth when she had told me that time passed us by more quickly as we grew older. The months were racing by now and life was very exciting. The Pathé newsreels were packed with images of our brave soldiers as they marched through tiny foreign villages. They all had cheeky grins and cigarettes dangling from the corners of their mouths. The girls all came rushing out to greet them with flowers and kisses. We stamped our feet and cheered as we watched. There was no bad news any more, just stories of victories and Mr. Hitler was on the retreat.

There was just one solitary cloud hanging over our otherwise happy home. Mum had often warned me that my short temper would bring me trouble, and once again she had been proved right.

I'd made the decision to destroy the evidence I had collected in my book of observations. Dad would be home soon, and I was now mature enough to appreciate the importance of my notes, and also old enough to fully appreciate just how much Mum had done for me, and also appreciate the sacrifices she had made. Unfortunately, when I raised the mattress to get at my book, it had vanished without trace. I knew immediately what had happened and I challenged Mum about it. She denied it, of course, but her denials were unconvincing. Later that evening, whilst still angry, I exacted my revenge.

I'm not sure what I was thinking when I did it, but I carried out my mission in cold blood and with military precision. I took a meat skewer from the knife and fork drawer, and crudely, but precisely I gouged out a set of initials on the right hand side of the wooden arms of the armchair.

'TB,

J

B.'

Mum was very angry when she discovered my act of apparent wanton vandalism. Her hand was raised, ready to punish me, until I pointed at the initials and shouted. "Tom Burke, Jacob and Buddy." Mum's angry face froze and then it crumpled like a plastic mask exposed to a flame.

She just sat there and cried like a baby, with her face on my shoulder. I wanted to say sorry and help her, but I was too young and I was helpless to assist her. I was filled with regret and remorse, but I couldn't undo what I had done.

We talked it over the following day and came up with a plan. If those initials were ever mentioned by my father, we would insist we knew nothing about them. The story was that they had been on the chair when it had first come into our house. It all sounded very easy, maybe too easy. I was painfully aware that I had, on several occasions folded under the pressure of cross examination. The war was drawing to a close, and those initials were threatening to undermine any promised celebrations.

When the end finally came, it was sudden and almost anti climatic. I sat at the radio and listened to stirring speeches from Mr. Churchill and King George. Mum and Mrs. Reilly went out with the other neighbours, and they all came home staggering around and singing. They were all very drunk. Somehow, someone hauled Mum on to the roof of the air raid shelter.

I watched as she danced with an imaginary partner, swaying precariously as she waltzed alone. Mrs. Miller had produced a gramophone and it was playing Temptation. I was worried that Mum was going to fall off as she danced with her eyes closed, holding on tightly to whoever it was inside of her head as she sang along.

You came, I was alone, I should have known
You were temptation
You smiled, luring me on, my heart was gone
And you were temptation
It would be thrilling if you were willing
And, if it can never be, pity me

The war was over, but nothing much seemed to change. We still had no money, rationing became even tighter and we waited and waited for news of my father. Mr. Churchill lost in the General Election and most of the other fathers were already home when Mum broke the news. She was seated at the dining table with the opened letter in her hands.

"Your father is coming home on Friday." She looked more anxious than pleased, but I decided it must have been my imagination. She took me in her arms and held me close.

"Thank you for helping me through Michael." Then she laughed. "Now the bloody fun starts."

I didn't sleep well on the Thursday night. I don't think any of us did. I was woken in the early hours by a strange noise. I crept downstairs and found Mum on her knees beside the armchair. She had a roll of sandpaper and was rubbing frantically at the initials I had carved on the arm. She looked up as I entered the room, mopped her brow, sighed and frowned.

"I can't shift them,"

"I doubt that Dad will ever notice them," I tried to look and sound unworried. I stood and watched as she applied a final coat of varnish to the wooden arm, and then we went back to bed.

I rose early, but both Mum and Mary were already up and running. I had a 'stand up' wash in the galvanized iron bath and Mum scrubbed me raw, pink and shining before dressing me in my Sunday best, and I commenced my vigil on the corner at ten o'clock. There were several false alarms during the course of my wait and then, at around mid-afternoon, the stranger came into view at the foot of the hill. I knew immediately it was him. He was carrying several suitcases and a kit bag, all of which he placed on the ground as he paused to light and then smoke a cigarette. Mum was hovering at the front gate, and I called out quietly. "He's coming." She gave a little startled cry and headed indoors.

He was on his way now and as he drew closer I could see him more clearly. He was wearing a grey check suit with a pale blue trilby hat. His suit was creased and crumpled, but his black shoes were very shiny. He was carrying a large green suitcase in his right hand. A pair of white Royal Navy peaked caps were dangling from the side, secured by a piece of string tied to the handle. Underneath his arm was a large piece of pink silk brocade material. In his left hand he held a smaller suitcase with a kitbag slung over his shoulder. I could feel my heart pounding as he came closer and closer.

"Michael?" He stood, studying me closely, his head tilted to one side.

I nodded. I felt sick with worry, and I felt uncomfortable.

"I'm your father. Come on then. Which one is our house?".

I led the stranger to the front door which was open. Mum was standing at the end of the hallway at the bottom of the stairs.

"Madge?" He asked querulously.

"Joe?" She replied. I had been expecting something more romantic than this, but it got even worse.

"Is there any chance of a cup of tea?" He stood in the hallway looking nervous.

"I've got one almost ready." Mum disappeared into the kitchen and Mary rapidly followed her.

I led Dad into the living room. He glanced around, nodding approvingly. "Very nice," he muttered, "very, very nice indeed." He sat down in my armchair, threw my cushion down on to the floor, and then shifted around until he was comfortable. He beckoned me to join him, and then lifted me up and put me on his lap. We sat in silence as we studied each other closely. He had very sad blue eyes, and he was unshaven. He smelt of stale tobacco and beer, and he looked nothing like the young man in football kit in the photograph I had treasured over the years. He rummaged in his pocket and produced a small, grubby white bag.

"Here, you used to like these when you were a baby." 'These' were sherbet lemons. They were still my favourites and I quickly stuffed a couple in my mouth. He glanced nervously over his shoulder in the direction of the door and lowered his voice.

"While I've been away," he lowered his voice even further until it was an almost inaudible whisper. "Has your mother been out with any other men?" It was the moment I had been dreading, and my father had only been in the house for a few minutes. I needn't have fretted about those initials, they were of no consequence.

There comes a moment in our lives when we suddenly grow up. This was my moment and an icy calm descended on me.

"No, never, not once," I was amazed at the feeling I managed to put into my voice. I jumped down from my father's lap just as Mum came in with his cup of tea, went outside and stood on the corner looking down the hill. Mum came out to join me a few minutes later and she took my hand. We stood together, side by side. It was one of those moments when silence feels right, but after several minutes Mum spoke.

"I love you Michael John," she said and she squeezed my hand.

"I love you too," I replied and squeezed her hand in return. I suddenly realised that all Mum had ever wanted was to be loved. It had taken me eight years to do so, but I had finally told her.

The war was over, my father was home, but I had this feeling that there were more battles ahead, but I now knew that wherever life took me, whatever life threw at me, I would always be just another boy from Bristol.

ABOUT THE AUTHOR

Born in Bristol in 1937, Michael Kelly was educated at St Mary on the Quay school, before moving on to St Brendan's College in Berkley Square, as one of the early successful 11 plus pupils at the end of the war.

A keen sportsman, Michael represented Bristol Boys at Under 15 level and played a solitary game for Bristol Rovers Juniors in 1954 prior to National Service, which was spent in the Royal Navy. He also represented Bristol United at rugby in season 1960/1.

Although well past retirement age, Michael is still working as a Commercial Insurance Broker and has no immediate plans for retirement.

18945191R00078

Printed in Great Britain
by Amazon